A Journey to uproot religion: & unlock the truth of Irish history

Mike Harper

Copyright © 2015 Mike Harper

All rights reserved.

ISBN: 1519627629
ISBN-13: 978-1519627629

If you would like to contact the author, please email us at

revivalwellinfo@gmail.com

www.revivalwell.org

No part of this book may be reproduced, stored in a retrieval system, or transmitted by any means without the written permission of the Author.

Scripture taken from the HOLY BIBLE, NEW INTERNATIONAL VERSION ®. Copyright © 1973, 1978, 1984 by International Bible Society. Used by permission of Zondervan Publishing House. All Rights reserved.

The 'NIV' and 'New International Version' trademarks are registered in the United States Patent and Trademark Office by International Bible Society. Use of their trademark requires the permission of International Bible Society.

"Scripture quotations taken from the Amplified® Bible,
Copyright © 1954, 1958, 1962, 1964, 1965, 1987 by The Lockman Foundation
Used by permission." (www.Lockman.org)

...Like a spinning top as it slows, do not lose balance by disobeying my words but be strong and devoted and in fear of me. The roots are like tentacles that will grab things, so if they are heaved out they will take other things with them. Climb up here with me and I will show you what is in this land. Before you stands a gate; the lock is rusted but I have a key...

1st Jan 2015

CONTENTS

Foreword	i
Chapter 1: Religion made Ireland sick	Pg 1
Chapter 2: Removing the stain of religion	Pg 14
Chapter 3: Religion made false claims to gain authority	Pg 21
Chapter 4: Christ as head	Pg 39
Chapter 5: Religion divided us	Pg 49
Chapter 6: A time for reconciliation	Pg 64
Chapter 7: Religion gave our inheritance to the enemy	Pg 73
Chapter 8: Take it all back!	Pg 87
Chapter 9: Religion led us to rebel	Pg 102
Chapter 10: Opening our eyes to see Jesus	Pg 121
Chapter 11: Religion sold us into slavery	Pg 131
Chapter 12: Your Children will ask	Pg 142
Chapter 13: Religion led us into pride	Pg 156
Chapter 14: An outpouring of humility	Pg 174
Chapter 15: Religion starved us	Pg 185
Chapter 16: A heart of stone	Pg 206
Chapter 17: Reconciliation	Pg 216
Chapter 18 From curses to blessing	Pg 221
Chapter 19: Identifying the religious spirits	Pg 227
Research Sources	Pg 232

Foreword

What has expanded into a six-month journey and also led to the writing of this book, began towards the end of 2014. For my wife Edith and I, it was a time of realising an approaching change in our lives and a lot of things were happening simultaneously. The pastor of our church, *Ministry of Jesus*, in Kilmainham, was travelling in December and had asked us to help out with the church schedule to keep it filled. We planned to hold a half-day of worship and invited some friends and the church members to come along. On the day, we arrived and set out some food and also had the sound system ready to go. A friend of ours arrived and led worship for about an hour but soon had to head off to a leadership meeting at his own church. For the rest of the event, nobody else turned up. Yet, something happened that day in my heart. I experienced a very powerful vision. In it, I was swimming out to sea and had gone really far, so far that I could no longer see the land. Then, for a moment, I grasped the width and depth of the sea and I became afraid because I did not know which direction to go. However, I immediately understood that I was being shown the width and depth of God's knowledge and revelation.

In the season leading up to this, I had become quite lazy in seeking revelation because I had felt that somehow I had learned everything! It sounds silly now to say that because, during the last six months, I have learnt so much from God about Ireland that would make what I was, anything but learned. I had previously been through several experiences with God and the only way I can describe these revelation experiences that took place is this, that I received a 'download' that was like a zip file that unpacked itself. These experiences had changed me dramatically and I knew that I had learnt so much from them. I even shared the experiences by writing small books and handing them out to people. Yet now here I was, with this sudden realisation about the vastness and depth of God. It was overwhelming. Yet, God wanted me to make a decision; He was asking me, "Which direction do you want to go in?"

I remembered a recent conversation that I'd had with a friend. We discussed how strong believers in Christ Jesus right across this nation are coming up against the 'brick wall' of religion. So I prayed and asked God to remove all religion from Ireland. Suddenly, the Holy Spirit brought to remembrance a vision that I had the very first time God began to talk to me about revival in Ireland, back in December 2012. In that vision, I saw Ireland as a holy mountain but on its side there was a stone pillar that needed to be cast into the ocean as it did not belong there. It did not originate there and it was having a corrupting effect on the mountain. This is what I wrote about it in 2012:

> *In a sixth vision, God took me on to the base of the mountain, where a great pillar had been constructed. And God said to me, "This does not belong. Smash it to pieces and cast it from my land." Then, with a rumbling sound, I felt the very earth shake all around me as God spoke in such power that it echoed to a great distance and proclaimed, "This is my land."*
> *[Extract from 'Be Revived: Prophecies & Revelations'[12]]*

However, at the time I believed that the corrupting pillar symbolised the stain of alcohol abuse on Ireland, knowing that alcohol has done a lot of damage in Irish society, influencing the health of many Irish people and resulting in family situations affected by alcoholism. Back in 2012 when a small group of us were meeting to pray for revival in Ireland, I thought that we were to pray so that pubs would close. Indeed, many people have prayed for this to happen and I still believe that, as a result, many pubs will close right across Ireland. Indeed I have had visions several times of pubs closing down and of cobwebs and dust filling them rather than people. What I am inferring here is that there would be more closures than what a recession could bring, that there would be a social move away from wanting to be in that kind of environment.

Although, theologically, you could argue that there is nothing wrong with a pub. However, I believe that you can also argue the opposite and say that God's judgement will come against the pubs. Why? It is because of them that so many wrong things are done and have been done in this land. Of course I am not leaving out the element of 'individual choice' but the simple fact is that, when people are under the influence of alcohol, they are easier prey to plans of the enemy – whether they are believers or not. I am not talking about abolition either because we know from America's example that it does not work. Nevertheless, Ireland as a nation has become known as a land of drinkers. This reputation is not because of our exports, it's because of our drinking. We need to see that reputation changed.

Ireland once had a very different reputation. We used to be known as the 'land of saints and scholars'. Now imagine for a moment, God removing our drunken image and restoring us to being a godly people living in a holy land where God manifests himself in such power that it changes the course of the whole world. That's what I believe God wants for us. He loves the Irish people and this land, and I believe that this land has a special place in His heart almost equal to that of Israel. Indeed, even speaking in secular terms, Israel is positioned at the centre of the world map and is also at the centre of a lot of news about conflicts and heated debates. Ireland too is a country whose people seem to gain attention right across the world. I am pretty sure an Irish pub can be found in almost every country. Irish people are welcomed wherever they go. Their accents are adored and their personalities are spoken of fondly and I believe that this is a blessing that God has given us as a heritage. However, everything God gives to us is ours for a reason.

My journey since December 2012 has not gone the way that I thought that it would. However, I remain content because in my heart I still have a burning hunger to seek God and to find out what He has to say. You might call me unconventional because, before I ever joined a church, I spent two years in the wilderness with God. When I went into that wilderness I was a mess, an alcoholic riddled with manic depression to the point where doctors wanted to give me a disability pension for life! I was financially broke. I was filled with shame over my choices in life. I felt that I had emotional scars the size of the Grand Canyon. Yet, when I came out of the wilderness, I had been washed clean, healed, trained, and anointed by God for service. In two short years He did an amazing work in my heart and then He sent me to join a local church.

Looking back now, I believe that this was for a number of reasons, not all of which are relevant to my testimony in this book. What is significant though is that, because of how God had trained me, I saw church from a new perspective, far removed from how I saw it when I was younger. Indeed as time went on, I began to believe that God wanted me to do something similar to what is recorded in Revelation:

> "Whoever has ears, let them hear what the Spirit says to the churches" [Revelation 2:29 NIV]

This calling to hear what the Holy Spirit is saying to the churches is a great calling but it is also a difficult one. Many Christians are not particularly interested in what is being done wrong. So far, in my experiences with God, I have received revelation concerning topics such as prayer and worship. To ask God to reveal His heart, and for Him to then share it is an amazing thing. But, for that to happen to a person like me, who deserves none of it, still amazes me. Over the past few weeks, God has begun a new work in me.

Going back to the event that I referred to, most Christians today, if they heard that nobody turned up would think that it was a failure! For me, it was no failure. I had such an amazing time just seeking God that I began to pray that nobody else would turn up! But after the vision, somehow the thought came to me giving me the idea that the pillar I had seen had nothing with alcohol. I began to consider the possibility instead that the stone pillar represented 'religion'.

After that day, I became drawn to a study of Irish history. Why? I didn't have a clue at the time but I browsed online and found a four and a half-hour video documentary made by the BBC and RTE called *'The Story of Ireland'*[1] which had originally been presented in one hour segments.

Whilst watching this history of Ireland, God began to reveal things to me at a level of revelation that I had not operated in previously. Most significantly, I began to understand not only the roots of modern-day Christian misconceptions of prayer and worship but also to understand why and how Ireland has gone through so much of a troubled past with its wars, terrorism, famine and drunkenness. The underlying cause weren't the foreign invaders or our own squabbling but instead religion and religiousness.

I mentioned already that there are godly people right across Ireland right now who are fighting for an awakening to come to this land. Indeed, if these men and women of God happened to be living in any other country, I believe that that country would have experienced that awakening in a very short time. Yet here in Ireland, it is as if they are up against an invisible force which blocks them from making the impact that they should be making. Quote often, it also drives them out of the existing churches. Why? It is because man-made religion has been allowed to manifest itself in Ireland like no other country. It exists in our churches, in our culture and our society. It has become *'a pillar upon a holy mountain that no one person can lift'*. But God, the Lord God Almighty, wants that rock to be thrown into the sea.

This is the start of a journey which I believe God is going to take us on in order to attack the roots of religion in Ireland. Some of them will be cut, some will be uprooted and others will wither. I could say that I am just one man and that I can't throw that stone pillar into the sea. Yet, through recent years, God has been establishing in me a gift of faith, and maybe it is so that I can complete this task for Him and other tasks too. I know that God can do this. I know that He will watch over us and give us strength. We yearn to see a mighty move of God in this land; indeed, God has already shown it to me! Perhaps that is why I will not agree to let it slip through our fingers. We must tear down religion! This prayer from Ezra is very relevant:

> "I am too ashamed and disgraced, my God, to lift up my face to you, because our sins are higher than our heads and our guilt

has reached to the heavens. From the days of our ancestors until now, our guilt has been great. Because of our sins, we and our kings and our priests have been subjected to the sword and captivity, to pillage and humiliation at the hand of foreign kings, as it is today. "But now, for a brief moment, the Lord our God has been gracious in leaving us a remnant and giving us a firm place in his sanctuary, and so our God gives light to our eyes and a little relief in our bondage." [Ezra 9:6-8 NIV]

Chapter One
Religion made Ireland sick
Church Mountain, County Wicklow

While I was watching the documentary on Irish history, a thought hit me as to why the Vikings had come to Ireland? You might think that was a very ordinary question. Indeed, if I asked it of any historian, he or she would probably tell me exactly as it had been explained in the documentary, that the Vikings lived an expensive lifestyle and so they had come to Ireland looking for fame and fortune. So let me re-phrase my question and put it this way. Why did God allow the Vikings to come to Ireland? There is enough evidence in Biblical records to show that when a country is obedient to the will of God, invaders may come but they will be overcome and defeated. The most likely truth, speaking from a Biblical point of view, is that what was going on in Ireland at the time was so bad that God allowed the enemy to come and attack the country in the hope that the people would change their hearts and turn back to Him.

This concept was strange to me at first. I love Ireland, and like many other Irish people, we have a certain respect for our history. This is not limited to Irish people alone. I remember from my travels to America and other places how believers all across the world talk about how

Ireland saved Christianity during the years 400-700. This, however, is in direct conflict with the concept that the Irish people had gone down such a wrong path that it had brought God's judgement on them. This happened not only once, but there has been a continual battering of Ireland and the Irish people all through the generations. If mistakes were made, that caused the people to turn away from God it must originate deep in our history. I wondered was there something that happened before the Vikings came that brought this judgement upon us.

Before I ever looked at this in detail, I thought that perhaps others before me would have gone to cut the religious roots. I thought that, perhaps, even Patrick the Apostle might have undone the spiritual roots of his time. I researched Patrick and realised that although Patrick did drive out the 'snakes' of his day, religious pagans, a brood of vipers, I discovered that the current corrupt man-made religion arrived in Ireland just before Patrick and would have only been in its infant stages when Patrick died. Patrick never got the opportunity to challenge it as his battle was against the paganism of his time and his ministry unlocked a powerful move of God in this land. However, I could tell that the main problem hadn't been dealt with as the Irish people still have stubborn religious hearts. You can see the fruits of it causing many problems in our modern churches, if you are willing to open your eyes and look.

Suddenly, what happened in the period of 400-700 became a great interest to me. The documentary had given me my first glimpse into what had gone wrong in our history. It had explained that, as the early Irish Church grew, people in its hierarchy became rich and powerful. Perhaps they even became abusive of their position and so I considered that it might have been a corrupt church that had brought destruction to our land. It certainly seemed plausible. I found myself launching deeper and deeper into a study of Irish history. I researched and researched until I became a 'sponge' that could hold no more. Then something strange happened to me.

Before telling you about what happened, I want us to go back to the very beginning of it all and look at the arrival of 'Christian religion' in Ireland. It began with a man called Palladius who was ordained by Pope Celestine in 431 and sent to be a bishop to the Christians in Ireland. This is the record of the first arrival of the Roman Christian religion to our shores. Historians have differing opinions about Palladius and the story of his life. Some argue that he never actually came to Ireland but went to Scotland instead. Others argue that he did come to Ireland and preached here for a time until the King of Leinster banished him, leaving Ireland, he then went to Scotland. This would certainly seem to be the more plausible story as there were churches in both countries that were claimed to be linked to this man, or at least to his disciples.

I will take a moment to point out a few observations. Firstly, there were already some Christian believers in Ireland before Palladius came. Perhaps these had migrated from Roman England or from elsewhere in Europe. Secondly, Palladius' mission to bring the Roman Christian religion to Ireland was essentially a failure. The historians agree on this point, recognising that Palladius' mission instigated by man failed because God had anointed Patrick for the task. Thirdly, there seems to have been a remnant of that 'man-made-mission' left behind in Leinster as Palladius, and/or his disciples, had established three churches in Wicklow which remained even after he left. Patrick arrived soon after Palladius and in some of his writings he mentions the fact of there being other churches in the land. But he made no claim of having any association with them. You could in fact argue that the pope had sent Palladius to Ireland but God had turned him away and, instead, had sent Patrick.

I carried out some research on these three ancient churches that were linked to Palladius. They were founded at Tigronry, Donard and Cilleen Cormac which is near Dunlavin. However, the precise location of two of these churches is unclear as all trace of them has been wiped away by time. There is only one known location left and is called Church Mountain and it is located in County Wicklow. This is the last remaining trace of when the man-made mission of religion first came to our shores. At the top of the mountain, the stones from an ancient cairn were re-assembled to form a church and remained in use as a pilgrimage site until 1798. It is unclear why pilgrims stopped going there, but it probably had something to do with the rebellion that was being fought that year. Perhaps the area was too treacherous to travel to and from at the time.

Now, let's take a step back to the strange thing that happened to me. As soon as I recognised the burden on my heart to seek God's words concerning the history of religion in Ireland, I became sick. Now, those who know me know that I do not get sick very often and, whenever I am sick, I try my best to turn to God, looking to Him first for healing and for comfort. One could explain very easily try to explain my sickness as it was at the start of the cold winter weather. But for four weeks, I went from one sickness to another and it was not just me who got sick but quite a few of my close family as well.

About half way through I was really crying out to God and asking Him why I was sick. I was led to watch a teaching by Rev. David Wilkerson that I'd found online entitled 'The Healing Power of Afflictions'[13]. In his sermon, David taught that God wants us to know that He is there with us through whatever we face as believers, that God is ordering our steps. It is one thing to understand such a thing theoretically or even theologically but it is quite another matter to actually live through such experiences. I came to realise that, in the midst of my illness, God was still there and was comforting me and helping me. I saw that God does not leave us alone in a darkened room but rather takes us up into His arms.

At the end of my third week of being sick, God reminded me about one of the things which was prophesied about this year, that God can speak to us 'out of the whirlwind' [Job 38:1]. I certainly felt as if I was in the middle of a whirlwind so I asked God to speak to me out of the storm that I was in. As soon as I did, God showed me that, just as sickness had come upon me, in the exact same way the sickness of religion had come upon Ireland. This is what He revealed to me:

> "Religion lingers like an illness that won't leave.
> First it takes away sight,
> Then it takes away energy and vitality.
> The words of religion are not spoken in faith but in weakness;
> The mouths of the religious leak the filth of unworthy chilled hearts.
> The voices of testimony are born vibrant but are wasted away
> Because religion does not produce an ongoing testimony.
> Religion keeps you from peace so that you don't rest but burn out;
> It makes hearts stubborn so that the Healer is not sought.
> It crept in the door like an unwelcome burglar who settled on a chair
> And the people just got used to him being there.
> They didn't even ask him to leave!
> Religion declares, 'Jesus is mine so follow me,'
> But, in truth, Jesus is Lord over all!"

Armed with this insight, and knowing that the sickness in my body (and in my family) would not go until we completed our first task for God on our prayer mission, Edith and I made plans to go to Church Mountain.

On the morning of that day, Edith had attended another meeting where a passage of scripture was read which had really struck her heart. As she read it out to me on the way to County Wicklow, I knew that it was relevant to our journey. We understood that we should read it out once we got to the top of the mountain and so we agreed that we would do that as well as reading the statement (above) about religion which God had given to me.

As we set off, we were very thankful to God that He had answered our prayers so that we would have a day of good weather. The sun was shining and there were only a few patches of cloud in the sky. Church Mountain is not far from Dublin and we travelled out along the road through Blessington until we passed the turn for Hollywood village. It was still morning when we started to climb but it was a beautiful morning. Some of the scenes that we witnessed driving to the location had been wonderful to see, but even more so now that we had arrived at our destination.

Photo: the path leading up Church Mountain

Before our trip, the Lord had already begun talking to me about the need to gather stones from the places where He would send us. You may ask why. Looking back, I can tell you that I didn't fully understand why either but revelation on it came at various points later in the prayer mission. For now, let me tell you a story from years ago when I took a couple of friends out to the side of a lake. It was back around the year 2008 or 2009. Back then, there was something that had been haunting me for years and I wanted to deal with it. Now, as I look back I have come to realise that as I picked up a stone and threw it into the lake, I was doing a prophetic act. I was declaring that, "This thing is gone from my life. It is now buried at the bottom of the lake never to resurface again." Then I encouraged my friends to do the same with their problems. What I didn't realise was that this act would have implications for the future and indeed for this mission for God.

I was being instructed that, as the prayer mission continued that we were to collect stones and throw them into the sea. This links back directly to the vision I had in 2012 about a rock which needed to be removed. This was something that I had kept to myself until our first trip and hadn't even shared with Edith yet. On the way up the mountain I kept on noticing bright white quartz stones. Some of them seemed to give off a shine which actually made them look as if they contained silver. Seeing these stones reminded me on the day of the special task that God was asking us to do.

Photo: Quartz rock found on Church Mountain

About half way up the mountain, we had to start guessing about which way to go. I had read some directions during the week on a blog that I had found online. It explained which path to take as the forest was a bit of a maze. According to the directions, at some point we were supposed to find a gap in the trees and be able to head straight from there to the top of mountain. This took a bit of searching but eventually we found a path that seemed to head straight to the top. Until then we had been walking on proper paths up a steady incline. Now things changed rapidly. Not only was the way steeper but it was also wet underfoot. There was even thorny vegetation that pierced through our clothing. As we climbed higher, the vegetation thinned but the ground continued to get wetter. We stopped halfway up the steep incline to take a quick break and recover our energy before continuing on. Soon after that I saw that, right at the top of our path, there was a barbed wire fence. I prayed and asked God to make a way for us and, soon after this, we came across another path leading to the left. We turned and followed this new path and from there found another trail going upwards to the top. Once again we saw a fence ahead but this one had been damaged by other hill-walkers and we easily got over the wire that had been trampled on.

Photo: summit of Church Mountain

As we neared the top, the path eased but the weather changed for the worse. The clouds were now big enough to block out the sunshine. The wind picked up and began to blow quite strongly. As we left the edge of the forest, we began to feel the elements fighting against our flesh much more than during the first part of the climb. However, by now we could now see the silhouette of piles of rubble on the top of the mountain. So we walked quickly onwards expecting to find a clear path over to the ruins of the church. Instead, the path that we were on seemed to be bringing us around the summit. So we took a risk and started to walk directly across the boggy ground towards the church. It is always a risk to walk across a bog as one could fall waist deep into cold murky water. I told Edith to keep her feet on high ground as best as she could as we walked onwards. Finally we made it. We went around the back of the church where we found some relief from the wind. Then, we climbed over the walls and into the church and sat down, again out of the wind.

Photo: ruins of the church

For Edith, I think it had been more of a physical struggle but, for me, I found it more of a mental challenge, always having to find the way forward. We sat there together, prayed and thanked God for the energy to have made it to the top and, amazingly, the sun suddenly broke out from the clouds and began to shine down on us whilst we prayed and prophesied. I read out the statement that God had given me about the roots of man-made religion being a sickness to the land. As this had been revealed to me through a sickness upon myself and my family, I knew that I had to make a declaration. I declared prophetically that the sickness in my body and in my family had come to an end. I also declared that the religion that has made my people sick, and my land of Ireland sick, that this too will come to an end. Then I read out the Bible verses that Edith had brought with her that day from the book of Isaiah. Where Zion was mentioned I replaced it with 'my people' and where Jerusalem was mentioned, I replaced it with 'Ireland'.

> "For *my people's* (Zion's) sake I will not keep silent, for *Ireland's* (Jerusalem's) sake I will not remain quiet, till her vindication shines out like the dawn, her salvation like a blazing torch. The nations will see your vindication, and all kings your glory; you will be called by a new name that the mouth of the Lord will bestow. You will be a crown of splendour in the Lord's hand, a royal diadem in the hand of your God. No longer will they call you Deserted, or name your land Desolate. But you will be called

Hephzibah, and your land Beulah; for the Lord will take delight in you, and your land will be married. As a young man marries a young woman, so will your Builder marry you; as a bridegroom rejoices over his bride, so will your God rejoice over you. I have posted watchmen on your walls, *Ireland:* (Jerusalem) they will never be silent day or night. You who call on the Lord, give yourselves no rest, and give him no rest till he establishes *Ireland* (Jerusalem) and makes her the praise of the earth. The Lord has sworn by his right hand and by his mighty arm: "Never again will I give your grain as food for your enemies, and never again will foreigners drink the new wine for which you have toiled; but those who harvest it will eat it and praise the Lord, and those who gather the grapes will drink it in the courts of my sanctuary." Pass through, pass through the gates! Prepare the way for the people. Build up, build up the highway! Remove the stones. Raise a banner for the nations. The Lord has made proclamation to the ends of the earth: "Say to *the daughter of the Irish people* (Daughter Zion), 'See, your Saviour comes! See, his reward is with him, and his recompense accompanies him.' " They will be called the Holy People, the Redeemed of the Lord; and you will be called Sought After, the City No Longer Deserted."

[Based on Isaiah 62:1-12 NIV]

After reading this, Edith led in prayer. But I remained stunned for a minute because the words from the verses 'remove the stones' had just hit me like a slap in the face. It was a confirmation of the task that God had been talking to me about and I laughed in amazement because, for some reason, I hadn't heard that part when Edith had read out the passage in the car. We continued to pray as the Holy Spirit guided us and then we began to make our way home. On the way back, I picked up a quartz stone and took it with me for the later part of the prayer mission.

Photo: *view from Church Mountain*

One thing really bothered me though. The mission of Palladius had been a failed attempt by the pope to introduce religion into Ireland but it did leave behind churches in Leinster. How could something that was seen as a failure, even by contemporaries of Palladius, leave a 'stain' of religion on the believers here in Leinster? I meditated and talked with God about this. I also wondered if perhaps I was being too harsh calling it a 'stain', that perhaps these churches had been doing a good thing, bringing the gospel of Christ to pagans. Indeed Paul spoke of a similar situation:

> "But what does it matter? The important thing is that in every way, whether from false motives or true, Christ is preached. And because of this I rejoice. Yes, and I will continue to rejoice" [Philippians 1:17-18].

My argument is actually not spoken in judgement of the churches, or indeed of the believers in those churches, but it is spoken against man-made religion itself. Indeed, the Roman Catholic Church in the fifth century may have been very different from modern day Catholicism. It may have been closer to what the true church should be but that does not mean that it was free of corrupting influence of men and women. If you plant an apple seed, will an orange tree grow? If you plant a potato, will a mandarin tree come up out of the ground? Look, therefore, at the 'tree of religion' which grew here in Ireland and then try to tell me that the seed that was planted in the beginning was free from man-made religion.

While I was thinking through these things, I began to realise that even though God was primarily speaking to me about Ireland, He was also speaking to me about my heart and indeed the hearts of all the Irish people. He did this because there is a day when religion arrives in our hearts. On that day we rebel against it fiercely but it still leaves a stain on our hearts which grows over time. I was reminded that when I was still a young boy, perhaps at the age of six, that I was being taken to church but I had to wear really uncomfortable shoes. You know the ones, black leather shoes that dig into your skin making it raw. Of course, I rebelled against having to wear those shoes. Perhaps in my heart I instinctively knew that God didn't care what shoes I wore. Maybe those shoes were to portray a certain image to other church members. Either way, I can say confidently today that God wasn't concerned with what shoes I had on. Yet I am left wondering, why do I still feel the need to put on 'good clothes' when I go to church?

It comes back to a question which I once contemplated with God as to why people go to church. If you visited a church and asked the people that question, probably everyone would give you a different answer. But, actually, there is only one reason why we should go to church or to meet with other believers, and that is to seek God together, listen to God, and then do what He says. What good does a finely pressed shirt do in the presence of God? It's in our hearts that He looks for cleanliness and not in our clothes. Remember the words of the prophet Joel:

> "Rend your heart and not your garments. Return to the Lord your God, for he is gracious and compassionate, slow to anger and abounding in love, and he relents from sending calamity." [Joel 2:13 NIV]

This is a powerful verse, indeed a promise that if we return to God, if we rend our hearts to Him then He will not send calamity. Sometimes, those of us who speak English do not fully understand the meaning of the Bible words that we use. So, here is the verse paraphrased:

> "Violently tear your heart into pieces and not your garments. Return to the Lord your God, for he is pleasant and kind (gracious) and shows sympathy and concern for us (compassionate), slow to anger and is plentiful (abounding) in love, and he abandons harsh judgement by finally yielding to a request (relents), saving us from a sudden event/disaster which will cause distress (calamity)."

It bothers me to think that man-made religion had planted its roots in my heart and in the heart of the Irish people. Most of us don't even realise it. Most of us don't even see it. But I declare the following words over myself and the Irish people: "See, your Saviour comes! See, his *prize for recognition of service* (reward) is with him, and his *compensation for harm suffered* (recompense) accompanies him" [based on Isaiah 62:11].

Chapter Two
Removing the stain of religion

When you look at the ministry of Jesus, we can see clearly Jesus address religious minded people, his disciple Matthew recorded the moment where Jesus addressed the Pharisees:

> "You snakes! You brood of vipers! How will you escape being condemned to hell?" [Matthew 23:33 NIV]

Why did Jesus use the word 'snakes' to describe the Pharisees? Think about it for a moment. What do snakes do? They bite people and inject them with a poison that kills them. The teaching of the Pharisees was poisonous and Jesus condemned it. This analogy is very similar to what God has been speaking to me about. He showed me that religion is like a sickness and that that sickness has been killing us! It is interesting to consider the so-called myth of Patrick driving the snakes out of Ireland. Many have suggested that perhaps they weren't physical snakes but instead it shows his opposition to the pagans. I would suggest that his action refers us back to the above Bible verse. This would mean that Patrick drove out those who were corrupted with the poison of religion, most of whom were the pagans.

I had been thinking about how religion may have seeped into my own heart. At this stage I already had been praying for God to rid my heart of any religiousness. I quickly realised that it's difficult for us to identify the exact day that religion arrived in our lives, and so it is difficult for us to find the root of religion in our hearts. After spending a lot of time trying to think and remember, I suddenly realised that if I knew what the stain of religion looked like, then perhaps I could follow a trail back to the root of it in my heart. This was easier said than done because, at this point, I did not know what the stain of religion looked like! For this reason I took my time and waited on God for the answers that I needed in order to fully understand what the stain of religion looked like. As I sought God He brought my attention to the story of the golden calf in the book of Exodus. The Bible tells us that Moses was up the mountain with the Lord receiving His commandments but, down below, the Israelites got tired of waiting for him to return and decided to make a calf out of gold:

> "When the people saw that Moses was so long in coming down from the mountain, they gathered around Aaron and said, "Come, make us gods who will go before us. As for this fellow Moses who brought us up out of Egypt, we don't know what has happened to him." Aaron answered them, "Take off the gold earrings that your wives, your sons and your daughters are wearing, and bring them to me." So all the people took off their earrings and brought them to Aaron. He took what they handed him and made it into an idol cast in the shape of a calf, fashioning it with a tool. Then they said, "These are your gods, Israel, who brought you up out of Egypt." When Aaron saw this, he built an altar in front of the calf and announced, "Tomorrow there will be a festival to the Lord." So the next day the people rose early and sacrificed burnt offerings and presented fellowship offerings. Afterward they sat down to eat and drink and got up to indulge in revelry." [Exodus 32:1-6 NIV]

I don't think that the Israelites were trying to turn back to the worship of one of the bull/cow gods that had been worshipped in Egypt because they had seen their God destroy every one of the Egyptian gods with the plagues. Instead, what I see happening here is that the people expected gods to be represented by statues that they could see with their own eyes. Certainly it had been that way back in Egypt as they would have seen the Egyptian god statues and symbols all over the land. I believe they used an image similar to what they would have known in Egypt, one of the Egyptian bull gods. They were discovering that their God was different to all the old gods. He was something new to them and so they made a new god. How would they make a new bull god? They knew that a new bull would be a calf and so they made a golden calf and credited it with all the great works that had happened in order for them to be brought out of Egypt. Even Aaron, who had also lived in the Egyptian culture amongst the images of their gods, fell into this trap and even facilitated the Israelites in its creation. But God saw what they were doing and told Moses that He was going to destroy them because of their idolatry. But Moses interceded on their behalf and God relented from His anger. Then Moses went down the mountain to the Israelites. He was dismayed by what he saw:

> "When Moses approached the camp and saw the calf and the dancing, his anger burned and he threw the tablets out of his hands, breaking them to pieces at the foot of the mountain. And he took the calf the people had made and burned it in the fire; then he ground it to powder, scattered it on the water and made the Israelites drink it. He said to Aaron, "What did these people do to you, that you led them into such great sin?" "Do not be angry, my lord," Aaron answered. "You know how prone these people are to evil. They said to me, 'Make us gods who will go before us. As for this fellow Moses who brought us up out of Egypt, we don't know what has happened to him.' So I told them, 'Whoever has any gold jewellery, take it off.' Then they gave me the gold, and I threw it into the fire, and out came this calf!" Moses saw that the people were running wild and that Aaron had let them get out of control and so become a laughingstock to their enemies." [Exodus 32:19-25 NIV]

What is clear to me from this whole event is that a remnant religious expectancy remained in the hearts and minds of these people who had spent all their lives in Egypt. All of them had been witnesses to the fact that God had torn down all the Egyptian gods one by one by the miracles which had set them free from their slavery. Yet a root of idolatry remained. Perhaps they observed how, in all other places where they believed in such gods, they made images of those gods and bowed down to them, thinking that they must do the same. It is amazing to think that they wanted to take a system of worship, which they had seen defeated before their very eyes and knew that it didn't work and apply it to what they wanted to do. Even more astounding is the fact that, while they couldn't wait to get free of Egypt, not wanting to be enslaved there any longer and were in complete rejection of what Egypt symbolised, yet here they were willing to adopt something from what they had previously rejected.

They were about to discover that God did not want them to make an image of anything in heaven or earth and then bow down and worship it. Their punishment came by the hands of the Levites who killed 3000 of those who had bowed to the golden calf. Even after Moses made intercession many others died of a plague that God had sent into the camp. Indeed this rule not to make a graven image is remembered by us in modern times as we study the Ten Commandments. It is interesting to note that, later on, when Joshua and the Israelites had crossed over into the Promised Land, they came across the 'holy' city of one of the Egyptian cow deities. Such was Joshua's distaste for the cow idol that when they took the city of Hazor [Joshua 11:13,21] they did not let anyone live and the so-called holy city was completely destroyed by fire. This was the only city that the Israelites totally wiped out in this way. The root of their actions comes from what happened previously at Sinai the mistakes which Israel had made there.

What we learn from these events is that:

- People carry forward expectations from the religion/culture that they lived in beforehand.

- People take those expectations and try to apply them to any new thing they do. Even when they already know that they don't work and even if they have rejected and rebelled against them, they try to apply them in the 'now'. This results in a mixing of the old idolatry with any new understanding of God and results in 'golden calf' worship.

- Mixing the old idolatry into the worship of God is seen by God as rebellion and therefore incurs judgement because God is holy and will allow no other gods to take His rightful place.

These findings might cause us to raise questions about our Christian heritage. For example, we could examine the life of Martin Luther and claim that anything that he started must contain at least some of the 'golden calf'. Meaning that, as he broke away and started something new, part of the old religious system that he had come from would be brought with him into the new. But when something new is started it doesn't have to be the case that we mix it with the old. Moses is a perfect example of this. Let's return to Exodus and see why:

> "When the Lord finished speaking to Moses on Mount Sinai, he gave him the two tablets of the covenant law, the tablets of stone inscribed by the finger of God." [Exodus 31:18 NIV]

You see, Moses went up Mount Sinai with blank tablets! He didn't go up there with tablets already written or even with tablets half-written. He went to hear what God wanted to say. He sought the standard that God required for His people. He obeyed God and allowed nothing of his own to influence the writing of the commandments, nor any corruption to sneak in inadvertently (perhaps in the way of his personal 'golden calf'). How many of us have ever truly approached God like that? How many of us have laid aside traditional church meetings and sought God for direction without applying any expectations or demands in order to hear what God has to say to us?

When we first become Christians we begin a journey of learning. At the beginning we are helped along by brothers and sisters in Christ, and also by our pastors and teachers. It is like the steady incline of a hill that we are climbing, where each step builds on the steps taken before. There is a similarity here to when Edith and I climbed Church Mountain. Up to a point in the climb we had followed the directions given by others which helped us greatly but, eventually, we ran out of instructions. In the same way we can reach a point where we don't know how to proceed further with our relationship with God. It's not that there is no way forward on our own but that, instead of having others to help us go any further, we must now find a way to move forward on our own. When we step out on our own, it is hard for us to know what to do. It is at this point that many believers stop and feel that they cannot go any further and so they gather with others who are in the same predicament and halt their journey. They will never reach the top of their 'mountain' unless they decide to leave behind those who are reluctant to move, and trust in God for the way to continue to the summit.

We sometimes go in roundabout-ways of getting to where we should be. Again, this is just like when Edith and I were trying to get to the top of Church Mountain and couldn't see how to get to where we needed to be. We went by an easy path that we could see in the hope that would take us there. These kinds of decisions in life are much more difficult than the earlier ones we took on our journey, back at the start of the hill. Some believers indeed decide to go back at this point, thinking that the way ahead is too difficult for them. Others get frightened and so they go back to repeat previous steps in the hope that they can get stronger by doing so. In fact, what we all need to do is to step out in faith and go directly to where God has instructed us to go. When you step out in faith, it means that you will overcome fear and be able to trust God fully as you take each step.

> "And without faith it is impossible to please God, because anyone who comes to him must believe that he exists and that he rewards those who earnestly seek him." [Hebrews 11:6 NIV]

There comes a time when we must take the truths that we learned at the start of our journey and begin to actually apply them in our daily lives. There is no point in just knowing the theory of something if you don't go on to experience it. There is no point in knowing how to pray with someone if you don't go and pray with people! There is no point in having spiritual gifts if you are not using them for the tasks that God has put before you. Your beliefs are not to be expressed just on a Sunday morning but God wants you to make your whole life into an expression of what you believe.

> "But you are a chosen people, a royal priesthood, a holy nation, God's special possession, that you may declare the praises of him who called you out of darkness into his wonderful light." [1 Peter 2:9 NIV]

I think that we must choose to give our whole lives to Jesus and then follow Him up the 'mountain' towards His goal for us with 'blank tablets' in our hands. The fight against religion will not just be in our land but also in our hearts. We have to ensure that we do not inject any false, man-made religion into what we do for God. If we do that, then we risk influencing the lives of other believers. In a sense, we would be like the snakes that I referred to injecting their poison into people. We don't want to stand before God on judgement day and answer for how others followed our teachings into falsehood. Let us always remain humble and have a teachable heart so that we may be brought to correction if and when we make mistakes.

As you read further in this book, you will hear more and more of our testimony about what God is saying about our religiousness. Please open your heart to how God might want to change you, to change your life, your ministry, your family, or even your church. It is easy to think, "Oh I'm not religious, that's those other folk down the road". But I ask, as your brother in Christ Jesus, to allow God to truly examine you as I have done during the last few months. This is a challenging thing to do. Stop reading and for a few minutes take this opportunity to pray and ask God to change you, to strip out any false religion or man-made religious roots that may exist in your heart. Allow God to change you, allow Him to correct you. Choose to no longer live in sickness but, realising the awful sickness that has been on the land of Ireland and, also in your heart, seek God for His remedy.

Chapter Three
Religion made false claims to gain authority
Kilashee & Kilcullen, County Kildare
Domnach Sechnaill, County Meath

There is something very striking about Patrick's writings as is especially seen in his confession and his letter to the soldiers of Coroticus[2]. Many scholars now believe these to be the only texts that can be reliably attributed to Saint Patrick and I would have to agree with them. Reading the confession of Patrick is, as my father told me, just like reading the book of Acts. Indeed it is an exciting text and I think that all Irish people should read it at least once in their life time. It is the testimony of an unlearned man who obeys the call of God to return to the very people who had enslaved him in order to bring them the goods news of Christ Jesus.

It is important to point out a few things at this juncture. After the death of Patrick and even for a good while afterwards, various groups continued to make claims about him. Their focus was to have their church, their relic, or their piece of land identified with him. Unfortunately, some of this involved the forging of documents which, in modern times, is being challenged. But those documents have in the past helped to form the legend surrounding Saint Patrick that is told around the world today. This brings me to make another point. Patrick himself became a legend as the myths about his life were multiplied.

Even now the legends continue to grow as yearly parades reflect huge international money making business. Sadly though, many parades no longer allow the message of Christ Jesus to be told and Christian organisations are often turned away, not allowed to take part. Year after year, the parades continue without little Christian input and many of the floats may even depict demonic or false god imagery. The day that originally celebrated the life of a humble, Holy Spirit-led man has become farcical! But, does this surprise us? We are warned in the Bible to boast only in Christ Jesus. Boasting in Saint Patrick rather than Christ Jesus has brought us to where we are today, celebrating the day with drunkenness and debauchery.

Furthermore, many places linked to Patrick's name (whether true or false) have become locations for pilgrimage. Even to this day, thousands of people go to places like Croagh Patrick in County Mayo. Edith and I climbed it last year but not for the same reason as others I would suspect. In truth, the legend of Patrick has become an attraction for domestic and foreign tourism and religious devotees. In a way, the people have made Patrick to be their 'golden calf'. This makes me sad as it is so far removed from the message of the real Patrick. If he were here, I'm sure that he would rebuke these pilgrim's for their idolatry. It is for this reason that we should be discerning about the Patrick legends and allow God to reveal to us the real truth.

When I read Patrick's confession, one event that he referred to really grabbed me. One morning, he awoke and felt as if a large stone had been placed on him and he could not move. He prayed to God and then the sun rose and, as soon as the light hit him, he was free. I believe that this was a prophetic event. The invisible stone that he could not see represented the lies and false claims that people would say about him after his death. It was only when the sun rose in the sky that he was set free and so, my brothers and sisters in Christ, I am praying that the Light of God will penetrate through all of the false claims and reach the truth about Patrick so that this stone may be lifted from him and his vision fulfilled.

Now let us recall two lines in the verse that God gave me about religion:

> "Religion declares, 'Jesus is mine', so follow me,
> But in truth, Jesus is Lord over all."

It is clearly evident that Jesus was not the only person that religious factions claimed to be theirs. Patrick was claimed by religion after his death when he could no longer protect himself. People made him out to be a great man. In reality, he was a humble man. His greatness was due to the power of God in his life. This is why we are told to boast only in Christ [1 Corinthians 1:31].

One of those apocryphal documents attributed to Patrick is known as *The First Synod of Saint Patrick*. This document also bears the name of two other men, Auxilius and Iserninus. Scholars debate the authenticity of this document; some believe that it is genuine but others believe that it was actually written at a time when the Leinster churches were trying to gain domination over the other Irish churches. A document linking Kildare with Patrick would certainly have helped them in any plea to the pope. This same rivalry for prestige was still going on between Kildare and Armagh in the seventh century. The argument seems to have been won eventually by the Armagh church by the year 640 with the help of a document of their own known as *'The Book of the Angel'*, which some scholars have called 'shameless propaganda'.

What we see here was a struggle for one church to control all the other churches in Ireland. Both the church of Kildare and the church of Armagh seemingly producing false documents with fake signatures of Patrick or of his contemporaries in order to gain favourable decisions from the pope that would give them primacy. In view of all this intrigue, a question must be asked. Why did any church want domination over all the others? The most likely answer is, is that which ever church won the prize would be able to impose a tax on all the other churches. That's right! The driving force behind this struggle was probably greed.

The First Synod of Saint Patrick was supposed to be a record of rules laid down showing how clergy should behave. However, if you read it, you will notice a clear distinction between this document and *The confession of Patrick*. I'm not referring to the type of Latin used or the style of writing. I am stating that there is a theological difference. Whilst *the confession* is the testimony of someone moving by the Holy Spirit, this document reads as if it was written by someone who wanted to restrict the moving of the Holy Spirit. Indeed, in several places I found it to be contrary to what Jesus taught us. It simultaneously attacks beliefs that people should hold to while guiding people towards ungodly actions. I have made a summary below to help us understand how to respond to this. What we witness here in this early religiousness are the same issues that we see infecting the church today.

The rules listed in *The First Synod of Saint Patrick* aim to restrain the development of these things:

- That like Jesus, we should aim to set captives free [Luke 4:18].
- That we should be free like the wind [John 3:8] to be guided by the Holy Spirit.
- That we should give our money as God directs us rather than depending on church authorities to spend it [Deuteronomy 26:12].
- That we should have freedom in worship, even to dance like David danced [2 Samuel 6].
- That we are to love our brothers and, if necessary, correct or rebuke them in the manner Jesus taught [Matthew 18:15-35].
- That we are free to start a church or ministry if God leads us to, because we are slaves to God rather than manly authority [1 Peter 2:16].
- That we should obey whatever God tells us to do, rather than being distracted by what others are doing, even if they oppose us [Philippians 1:15-18a].

Instead, *The First Synod of Saint Patrick* wrongfully intended to guide believers to:

- Seek money, *but...*
  the Bible warns us not to toil to acquire wealth [Proverbs 23:4].
- Serve church authority, *but...*
  the Bible says that we must serve God alone [Luke 4:8].
- Correct our behaviour, *but...*
  the Bible shows us that the cause of our sinful behaviour is our hearts and that it is our hearts that need correction [Matthew 5:27-28].
- Have an acceptable appearance, *but...*
  the Bible stresses the importance of inner beauty [Psalm 51:6, 1 Peter 3:3-4].
- Judge others and assign to them a punishment, *but...*
  the Bible shows that only God is able to judge righteously [Psalm 9:7-8].
- Avoid provision from non-believers, *but...*
  the Bible allows it as long as God is glorified and no one's conscience is affected [1 Corinthians 10:27-33].
- Make vows, *but...*
  the Bible discourages vows, showing how it can leave us under the enemy's influence [Matthew 5:33-36].
- Allow church authorities to take money for themselves from the church , *but...*
  the Bible warns us about the danger of robbing God [Malachi 3:8-10].
- Make simple things complicated. For example, requiring a forty day wait before baptism, *but...*
  New Testament baptism was immediate, on profession of faith [e.g. Acts 8:35-39].

- Make choices to put people into positions of authority, *but...*
  it is the Holy Spirit who should ordain or anoint people for service [1 Corinthians 12:11].
- Teach that the church is the building, *but...*
  the New Testament word 'church' means the believers, those who are called out by God [e.g. Colossians 1:18, 24].

At the time of the synod, the common punishment for breaking the rules was excommunication from the church. However, to be refused admission to church means nothing if we are united with Christ and one body with all true believers [1 Corinthians 12:13 & Ephesians 4:25].

At this point it is important to look at three figures of Irish history: Auxilius, Iserninus and Secundinus. These three men according to some records were bishops and close associates of Saint Patrick and one was even supposed to have been his nephew. Yet as we have said, a lot of documentation after Saint Patrick's death was actually forged. So what do we know for sure? We know that these men were sent to Ireland in 438 by Germanus. Their arrival in 439 was recorded in the Irish Annals stating that they had come to Ireland to assist Patrick. I believe, as do others, that this is where things got confused. Remember that Palladius had arrived in 431 on a mission on behalf of the Catholic Church. But here in Ireland, Palladius was known as Patricius.

So, one theory is that these men did not actually come here on behalf of the Catholic Church to help Patrick, but instead to assist with the mission that Palladius had begun. This makes even more sense when we consider the fact that the three men set up their churches in Leinster. Auxilius established a church at Kilashee in County Kildare while Iserninus set his church up at Kilcullen, also in County Kildare. It later became a monastery. Secundinus established his church at Domnach Sechnaill in County Meath, known today as Dunshaughlin. If these men had indeed come to Ireland to support Patrick, would we not find their churches in the north or the west of Ireland where Patrick mostly operated? Instead we find them located in Leinster and within reach of the three churches of Palladius.

The sketch map below demonstrates how close they were. All were within a day's walk of each other and for some of them you could walk to another and back in one day. As newcomers to the island, perhaps the three friends wanted to stay within reach of each other for mutual support.

It is also worth mentioning that near to Dunshaughlin is the town of Trim which also has historical importance. There was a monastery built there by Lommán, who was also supposed to be a nephew of Patrick. I am not sure how many 'nephews' that Patrick is supposed to have had but, as I my research, I certainly seemed to be finding more and more of them. This is why it is important not to take too much notice of those who made grandiose claims about Patrick's heritage, but instead to focus on the truth and also on what makes sense. It is quite likely that the church in Dunshaughlin was responsible for planting the church at Trim. Indeed, the method seemed to have been to train disciples and then to send them on to begin a ministry in another place but always within easy reach of where they had come from. We must remember that travel between places was not just difficult but dangerous, especially if they had no letter or commendation from a known authority. Passports did not exist yet! If you arrived in a town where you were unknown, you could be treated with great suspicion and badly treated or worse. Perhaps that is why these church planters did not venture too far from each other.

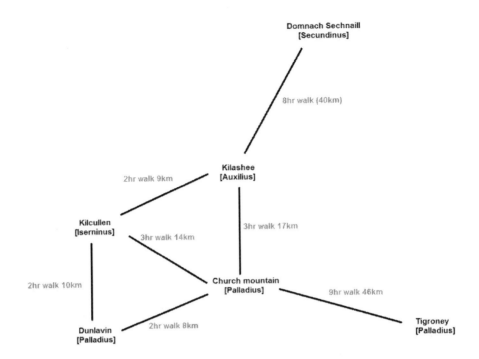

Map: sketch showing the relationship between the churches in Leinster

As Edith and I sought God about these things, some very important pieces of revelation were given to us. This started with us being guided to various passages in Paul's letter to the Galatians:

> "Formerly, when you did not know God, you were slaves to those who by nature are not gods. But now that you know God—or rather are known by God—how is it that you are turning back to those weak and miserable forces? Do you wish to be enslaved by them all over again? You are observing special days and months and seasons and years! I fear for you, that somehow I have wasted my efforts on you."

> "For it is written that Abraham had two sons, one by the slave woman and the other by the free woman. His son by the slave

woman was born according to the flesh, but his son by the free woman was born as the result of a divine promise. These things are being taken figuratively: The women represent two covenants. One covenant is from Mount Sinai and bears children who are to be slaves: This is Hagar. Now Hagar stands for Mount Sinai in Arabia and corresponds to the present city of Jerusalem, because she is in slavery with her children. But the Jerusalem that is above is free, and she is our mother."

"Now you, brothers and sisters, like Isaac, are children of promise. At that time the son born according to the flesh persecuted the son born by the power of the Spirit. It is the same now. But what does Scripture say? "Get rid of the slave woman and her son, for the slave woman's son will never share in the inheritance with the free woman's son." Therefore, brothers and sisters, we are not children of the slave woman, but of the free woman." [Galatians 4:8-11, 22-26, 28-31 NIV]

"It is for freedom that Christ has set us free. Stand firm, then, and do not let yourselves be burdened again by a yoke of slavery."

"You who are trying to be justified by the law have been alienated from Christ; you have fallen away from grace. For through the Spirit we eagerly await by faith the righteousness for which we hope. For in Christ Jesus neither circumcision nor uncircumcision has any value. The only thing that counts is faith expressing itself through love. You were running a good race. Who cut in on you to keep you from obeying the truth? That kind of persuasion does not come from the one who calls you. "A little yeast works through the whole batch of dough." I am confident in the Lord that you will take no other view. The one who is throwing you into confusion, whoever that may be, will have to pay the penalty."

"You, my brothers and sisters, were called to be free. But do not use your freedom to indulge the flesh; rather, serve one another humbly in love. For the entire law is fulfilled in keeping this one command: "Love your neighbour as yourself." If you bite and devour each other, watch out or you will be destroyed by each other. So I say, walk by the Spirit, and you will not gratify the desires of the flesh. For the flesh desires what is contrary to the Spirit, and the Spirit what is contrary to the flesh. They are in conflict with each other, so that you are not to do whatever you want. But if you are led by the Spirit, you are not under the law."

"But the fruit of the Spirit is love, joy, peace, forbearance, kindness, goodness, faithfulness, gentleness and self-control. Against such things there is no law. Those who belong to Christ Jesus have crucified the flesh with its passions and desires. Since we live by the Spirit, let us keep in step with the Spirit. Let us not become conceited, provoking and envying each other." [Galatians 5:1, 4-10, 13-18, 22-26 NIV]

As a result, we travelled to what remains of the churches that were built at these three locations, reading out the words of God from the above passages and praying as the Holy Spirit led us. I was most surprised by the position of the round tower at Kilcullen I am pretty sure that from that high place Church Mountain could be seen. I could not tell for certain because of low cloud cover on the day. But nevertheless I realised how close these places really were to each other. At Kilashee, we found access to be a problem as the tower was in the middle of a building site behind the hotel. A fifteen-foot wall was separating us from the tower. We did manage to find our way through the hotel grounds to a place which had rubble on the ground and was in between the tower and a graveyard and we prayed there. At Dunshaughlin, we found the old arch which stands in the grounds of a more recently built Church of Ireland building.

Photos: Kilcullen(top left), Kilashee(top right) and Dunshaughlin(bottom)

However, even with all the praying and travelling around, I felt like our venture was incomplete, that I perhaps needed more understanding. As I prayed and talked to God about this, He prompted me to do something very unusual and seemingly completely unconnected. I was prompted to switch on my game console and to play a football game on it. I don't know which I found stranger, the request or the realisation that I hadn't played this game for more than three years. I switched it on and followed what the Holy Spirit was leading me to do which was to set up and manage a team but not to play any of the matches. I just had to sit back and see what happened as the computer played matches.

This is my record of what happened:

> *As I sat back and watched, I saw weakness but I had hope*
> *Because I wanted to see what God would do.*
> *The first game played; it was a draw and the second one too.*
> *I was getting unsettled; I wanted my team to win.*
> *Then, in the next match my team seemed to be losing so I quickly stepped in -*
> *I took control and tried to fight but it had gone too far and so the game was lost*
> *For the next game, I came prepared and I got a few goals into the lead;*
> *Then I let the computer play again instead of me,*
> *But immediately they started to lose and so I took the reins again and won.*
> *So, for several more matches, I played on and won each time.*
> *Already I was thinking of strategies:*
> *'Who could I get in to strengthen the team?*
> *What formation changes could I make?*
> *What player transfers might be needed to strengthen the weaknesses?'*

My dear brothers and sisters in Christ, I hope that you are picking up the significance of what was revealed to me by doing this. Here is a summary of what I learned. I have broken it down into steps for you. It illustrates how religious authority creeps into the hearts of all of us:

1. God told me to do something by asking me to start a team, but when I started, He seemed to want me to do nothing but to wait on the Lord and see what He could do. I was supposed to learn that, if it's His promise, then He will fulfil it.
2. Things are going smoothly until I see a turn to what I think is the wrong direction. I take control of the situation to try and fix it but it results in failure.
3. Not liking the results, I take more control and try to get it back to how I think it should be but the situation moves again to what I perceive as failure. From then onwards, I refuse to let the issue go.
4. I take full authority and begin to plan what I perceive as better ways to run things. I think how can I adjust people and

situations in order for the team to reach where I think they should be.

This is the exact same thing that we see happen in churches and ministries today!

You may ask, "What is wrong with authority in the church?" What has authority to do with religiousness? Examine the diagram below that shows a cycle of events that takes place. You will see that it explains a lot of what is happening in our modern churches and answers the question as to why there are so many denominations. It describes a system where man has taken control. To see how this contrasts with God's word, read these verses:

> "Trust in the Lord with all your heart and lean not on your own understanding; in all your ways submit to him, and he will make your paths straight. Do not be wise in your own eyes; fear the Lord and shun evil." Proverbs 3:5-7 NIV

The cycle need not be endless but can be broken at the point of 'Nothing happens'. To do so at this point we must not to yield to the temptation to keep in control. Instead, we must submit to God and go even deeper with Him and follow His leading. Remember that whatever is planted at the beginning will only grow more of the same. If you want men to control things, then plant religious seed. If you plant the seed of God in control and stay in submission to Him, then He will do amazing things. This takes determination and strength. Many of us have become so corrupted by the cycle of religion. Because it has existed for so long, we don't realise that there is a better way open to us.

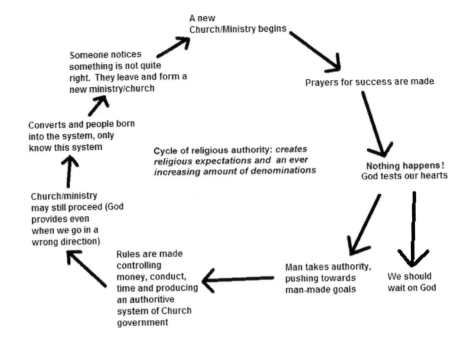

Diagram: The Cycle of Unending Denominations

If you look at people caught up in this kind of system, you will realise that they become dependent upon the leadership of their church for instruction and everything else that they need. However, a pastor is not an unlimited resource. Imagine for a moment that the pastor is a cow who feeds her calf. Now see her calf getting bigger and bigger, but always looking for more milk and never actually learning to get nourishment from the same source that the cow gets it from. That calf would wear out its mother to death! So many pastors are overwrought but God, on the other hand, is a never ending source of everything that we need [Psalm 46:1, Matthew 6:11].

We need to remember that believers are not part of an organisation in the first place but we are members of a family. We are actually co-heirs in the inheritance that Jesus has won for us [Romans 8:17]. We are children of God and brothers and sisters in Christ. Each of us is equal in authority and position. Where Christians differ is in the anointing upon them, their gifting and the obedience to the call of God in their lives. The church is a family and God is the Father of the family. Imagine Him bringing a new baby son home. In the family there is already an older brother who has been there eight years. The older brother feels like he knows a lot more so will try to help the younger brother find his way. However, the older brother must never claim that he has authority over the younger brother. Sure, at the start, he does know more and certainly has a right to feel senior. But, this seniority is not for authority. Instead it is for protection and love. Over time, the younger brother will catch up. If he has a hunger for more knowledge then he could even surpass the wisdom and understanding of the older brother. The older brother must remain humble and even hope that his brother will rise to reach further than he. Consider the account of Elijah and Elisha. Elijah selected him [1 King 19:16] brought him alongside to disciple him and then, at the right time, he blessed him and Elisha received a double-portion anointing from God. I heard it said somewhere that a good leader makes leaders of others. The authority in the family is centred in God the Father. Things have gone astray in the past and in the present Christian church because people have either claimed or interrupted that authority. Foolishly we have allowed it.

How that authority gets claimed is very important. In Patrick's time people simply made claims saying, "Patrick came here", "Patrick owned this" or "This is Patrick's nephew". These days it is quite often done the same way but by making claims about what a person can do. They might say, "This person has a healing ministry", or "This person has brought millions to Christ". Indeed, modern churches often use such things as advertising. They might say, "Come to our church this Sunday. We have a preacher coming who has an anointing for giving prophetic words!" People fall for this and rush to get there in the hope that they might hear a prophetic word for their life. By doing so, in effect they are saying, "This person is an authority who I want to speak into my life." Where does this leave us in regards to seeking the true authority, God the Father? He is able to give you a prophetic word that surpasses anything any other person could possibly say to you. God is the source and any other source is extremely limited. God has the power to give you a prophetic word every day, a healing every day or a miracle every day. He could give to you even seventy miracles a day if you needed them and trusted Him for them. My brothers and sisters in Christ, don't run from one 'cow' to the next just because its 'milk' might taste sweeter! Instead find the real source and take your fill at the Lord's Table [Psalm 23:5, 34:8, John 6:53-54].

What we find from Church history is that once authority is accepted, rules will be given for you to obey by those whom you have allowed in authority over you. Remember these words:

> "It is for freedom that Christ has set us free. Stand firm, then, and do not let yourselves be burdened again by a yoke of slavery." [Galatians 5:1 NIV]

A set of rules given by a human authority may seem wise to you. They may even seem to line up with scripture. That does not mean that those rules are for you and they can actually be hazardous to you if you go by them. Sin can be defined simply as disobedience of what God has instructed us to do. Imagine for a moment a church with one pastor and with a hundred people in the congregation. Do you believe that one man could understand the plan, the calling and the instructions that God has for each of those one hundred people and on a daily basis? Now, imagine three men, John Jack and Jim, each of them attending that church. God wants the three men to study the Bible and pray but each on a different day of the week and in their own homes. However, the church organises a Bible study on a Tuesday. The three men attend the study and listen to what a teacher has prepared for that time. Those three men then feel that the Bible study has filled their allocated time for study of the Word of God and so they ignore what God requested. They are now acting sinfully by attending the Bible study and neglecting God's command. If you attend church if God wants you to be in some other place, you are acting in sin!

We must accept that a human being in authority cannot possibly know everything. Such a person cannot make plans and rules that are complex enough to fit around what God has planned for each individual in the church. The Book of Proverbs, as mentioned before, tells us to submit to God in everything we do. That is an individual calling out to God to find out what God's planned steps for them are. When something is organised, we must ask, "Is this right for me?" rather than just nodding in submission to the human authority. It adds up to this: when humans take authority in the church, it can very easily lead people into sin simply because man cannot comprehend the mind of God. Looking at the church of today, we must ask, "Where has the fear of the Lord gone?" I don't know about you, but I want to learn how to stay in the centre of God's will for my life.

Most of the time, it's likely that God will require you to go to church on a Sunday. It's also likely that He will send you to the Bible study and the prayer meeting. But don't you want to be certain about His leading? It requires you to be asking a question to God on a regular basis: "Lord God, what do you want me to do today? I want to do your will!"

When the modern churches branched out to form local groups and denominations, there was a lot of criticism of the Catholic Church and perhaps there still is from time to time. Yet people remain blinded to the fact that they have simply adopted exactly the same system as what Catholics have. Sure the theology is different, but the churches are still operating under the same religious rules that can lead to a spiral of disaster. We only have to look at our past to see where this can take us. The churches of Kildare and Armagh fought it out in the eighth century, making false claims in order to gain power, money and authority over the whole church of Ireland. God was saying this to them;

> "Put to death, therefore, whatever belongs to your earthly nature: sexual immorality, impurity, lust, evil desires and greed, which is idolatry. Because of these, the wrath of God is coming. You used to walk in these ways, in the life you once lived. But now you must also rid yourselves of all such things as these: anger, rage, malice, slander, and filthy language from your lips.

Do not lie to each other, since you have taken off your old self with its practices and have put on the new self, which is being renewed in knowledge in the image of its Creator." [Colossians 3:5-10 NIV]

My brothers and sisters in Christ, realise this, the wrath of God came on our land! In the same century that greed corrupted the churches of Ireland (take note that greed=idolatry), God allowed the Viking marauders to come here. They landed here in 795 and attacked churches up and down the country, and stole the wealth that had been acquired through greed.

I ask you, Lord God, have mercy on my land and upon my people. Teach me, indeed teach all of us to break free from religion and walk in your freedom. Help me to get rid of every detestable root of religion from my heart. In Jesus name, amen!

> **Note to church leaders** – *if you have found what I have written offensive, then I beg of you to think about the throne of God in Revelation. The twenty-four elders removed their crowns and placed them at the feet of Jesus. Your crown is your authority. However, it is also that burden of responsibility caused by all those people looking up to you. Now is the time to take your crown off and lay it at the feet of Jesus. God is calling you to worship him. The choice is yours!*

Chapter Four
Christ as head

If man-made religion is seeking to claim authority over us, then it's important for us to know the truth and put Jesus as the authority in our lives. He is not just the head of the church [Colossians 11:3], but also the head of every man [1 Corinthians 11:3]. But, what does being the head mean in reality? By definition, the head means the upper part, housing the brain and the sense organs. It can also refer to someone who holds the leading position. With this in mind, every person must look to Jesus for direction and leading and put Him first in everything. The same principles apply to the church. Let us consider what Jesus said about being our shepherd:

> "I am the good shepherd. The good shepherd lays down his life for the sheep. The hired hand is not the shepherd and does not own the sheep. So when he sees the wolf coming, he abandons the sheep and runs away. Then the wolf attacks the flock and scatters it. The man runs away because he is a hired hand and cares nothing for the sheep. "I am the good shepherd; I know my sheep and my sheep know me— just as the Father knows me and I know the Father—and I lay down my life for the sheep. I have other sheep that are not of this sheep pen. I must bring them also. They too will listen to my voice, and there shall be

one flock and one shepherd. The reason my Father loves me is that I lay down my life—only to take it up again. No one takes it from me, but I lay it down of my own accord. I have authority to lay it down and authority to take it up again. This command I received from my Father." [John 10:11-18 NIV]

In the above passage of scripture, Jesus is speaking about Himself as the Shepherd of the sheep. He tells us that there will be one flock and one shepherd, meaning Himself. Peter, teaches in his first letter, explaining that being a church leader is like being a shepherd. After all, we are meant to follow in the steps of Jesus. Jesus is the 'one shepherd' of the flock, but those who are called to be pastors function as under-shepherds. Thus, the original truth remains, and Jesus remains both as head of the church and head of each individual man. In teaching others to be shepherds, Peter gave them instructions about the task and the required standard [1 Peter 5:2-5]:

- To do the job willingly and not out of obligation
- Not to pursue dishonest gain
- Be eager to serve
- Not to 'lord over' others
- Be good examples
- Be clothed with humility

These are essential attributes and I think that every pastor should have them. However, we have to admit that many modern pastors are failing in one or more of these areas. Indeed, one often encounters negative reactions when a prophetic person makes an attempt to correct a pastor in one of the areas mentioned. When that happens, it does not go down too well as many pastors do not take correction easily. If this is the case, then surely the pastors have become too proud but perhaps this is not entirely their fault. Remember, it was the people who made a golden calf and worshipped it. In the same way, people have made pastors of the modern church to be their 'golden calves'. They look to them for all of their guidance and instruction and somehow forget that Jesus is the true head of the church.

A pastor is not meant to be a person whom others will follow for the rest of their lives. Instead the pastor's role is to help new believers become mature Christians. These mature Christians will then be able to hear the word of God for themselves and Jesus, their head will direct them. They may remain in the flock to help it grow, or be sent by Jesus to reach the world with the gospel. That is how things should be but it is not how things currently are in many churches! Many people spend their whole lives in the same church, sitting in the same seat, from childhood to death, maybe even outliving several pastors, but never coming to maturity. This problem occurs when people assume that the pastor is their head and, if their head hasn't asked them to do anything in particular, then they believe that they are still on the right path. Remember, Jesus as the Living Word is always speaking [John 1:14-18] and all we have to do is listen and obey. This is where the distinction lies. Mature Christians listen to Jesus and obey. Immature Christians depend on their pastor.

Let us all repent for all the times when we have boasted to others about our pastors instead of talking about Jesus [1 Corinthians 1:31]. Let us repent for not maturing under our pastor's leadership for year after year. Let us repent for allowing such things to continue unchecked in our churches. Let us repent for the greed for power and authority that has continued unchallenged in our churches. Then, after we have repented, let us seek God for the changes that are needed. Let us learn how to be humble pastors and teachers fulfilling the role of helping our brothers and sisters into maturity. Let us not be the kind of people who are happy that others are in the room to hear our sermon, but are glad to see it if nobody turns up to hear our sermon because they have gone and started their own churches. Let us stop producing 'church' in the religious sense and start producing the real church – made up of mature men and women of God who listen to God above all others and follow Him wherever He leads them at whatever cost.

As we move forward, we must counter-act the rules that religion has forced on us because we allowed the wrong authority to rule in our lives. I have put together a list of things which we must strive to see restored and maintained in the church:

- Just as Jesus came to set captives free, to give sight to the blind, to proclaim freedom to prisoners and to give good news to the poor [Luke 4:18], we need to follow the same pattern. This is what Jesus ministry was about and He has not changed. In response, we need to allow Him to do a work in our lives and enable us to have the strength and boldness to set captives free. Doing this does not need the consent of your pastor or elders. It is the call of God for all of us to fulfil this mission. If you ask God for guidance, then He will give opportunities to you. He will even send people who need help to your door.
- To follow leading of the Holy Spirit, learn from Him, and allow Him to remind you of the things you have learnt while growing into maturity [John 14:26]. We must put the guidance of the Holy Spirit above our church 'programmes', and obey what God is telling us to do. I remember hearing a story about a girl who saw a vision of a cabbage. Not knowing what to do with a vision like this, she mentioned it to her friend who told her that she had seen a cabbage in a dream. As a result, they both decided to go to a nearby shop and buy a head of cabbage. On the way the Holy Spirit prompted them to go and witness to a street musician. They obeyed, and that man responded by giving his life to God. How many times have we discounted the small signs, the prompts, the dreams and visions that the Holy Spirit has given us! Let us not turn away from heeding these things anymore.
- Give as God leads us to give. In the Old Testament, the people were instructed to give tithes to God. However, in the New Testament, every part of our lives is to be given over to God [Romans 12:1-2]. In the Old Testament, people were to allow God to guide them as to who they should give their tithe to, whether it be to a Levite or foreigners, or to the fatherless or to a widow [Deuteronomy 26:12]. In the New Testament every believer is a Levite, as they are called a royal priesthood [1 Peter

2:9]. Many people forget this and only give to their church's weekly collection. However while God will lead you to give to your church, He might also lead you to give your money to a missionary half-way around the world!

- We must move from our comfort zones and be free in the way we express worship. I have already written a book about this topic entitled *In Spirit and Truth*$_{14}$. It is vital for us to express our love for God in worship. However, displaying our love is not always a pretty sight. There may be tears. There may be dancing or other elements. We must stop allowing others to merely lead us into singing songs while calling that worship. Instead, we must be active in seeking God through our worship and to express our love for Him by singing words from our hearts. Worship is all about meeting with God, sacrificing the desires of our hearts on the altar so that we may be changed. If you are not changed during a 'worship time', then you have not been engaging in worship but have just been singing!

- We must love our fellow believers as brothers and sisters in the way that the Bible teaches us. It is always easier for us to 'lord' over those around us who, in our estimation do not come up to the mark. We are to love these brothers and sisters because if we don't, then it is a sign that we don't even love God [1 John 4:20]. Let us be humble before others just as Christ was, not easily judging them but instead coming alongside them, giving support and praying for them. God may even require us to lay down our lives for them [1 John 3:16]. We must always remember that we are not perfect people, and even now, when we have been undergoing the renewal of our minds, we still fall short of glory of God's righteous standards. It is only the blood of Jesus that has saved us; it is only because of God's mercy and grace and not because of anything that we are in ourselves.

- We must listen to God for direction before starting a ministry. We must wait for God to appoint us for serving Him [1 Tim 1:12]. Within traditional church structures, people often drift into ministry, into any opening that comes their way. A person could even be in a ministry that God never even called them to do! Only God can truly ordain and anoint people to do the work that He has set out for them to do. They do not need approval from men in the first place; they just need the call and commission from God. Churches need to become centres where people are enabled to carry out what God has called them to do. They should function as 'apostolic centres'.

- We must serve God only and obey God before men [Matthew 6:24] [Colossians 3:23]. This is linked to the previous point, but it involves a principle that needs to be stated clearly. Christians should respect and follow the leading of their pastor until they reach maturity in Christ. At that point, they really need to seek God on their own behalf so that they can move further into the particular purpose that God has ordained for them. You see, the primary responsibility of a pastor is not to start a church and fill it but, instead, to train and equip the flock so that they reach maturity [Ephesians 4:12]. If a flock reaches maturity quickly then their pastor is doing a good job. However, the opposite may also be true. Maturity simply means that a person has learnt to listen to God personally and to obey Him fully, having given their life over to Him to such a degree that they no longer live, but Christ lives in them [Deuteronomy 13:4, Galatians 2:20]. A mature person, therefore, does not need to go and listen to endless sermons, but rather follow the call of God. The pastor, instead of being possessive, should be filled with joy when a mature person leaves in order to follow God to another place for it means that he has been successful in what he was called to do. Why, then, do some pastors look at an empty seat after a person leaves and regret their going? In the same way, a pastor should be glad if a mature person stands up in church and says 'God is leading us to do such and such', because it means that God maybe anointing them for a new ministry within that church. Read Thessalonians 1:4-8. It shows the correct way to release brothers and sisters chosen by God for service. In this case they became a model to other believers by first being imitators of their teachers and of Jesus Christ. Why, then, do some pastors react negatively saying, "If God wanted you to do that, then He would have told me about it first?" That is not how God works. A pastor cannot hear the calling that others have on their lives. God calls people individually by name; the pastor hears his own calling and only his. If he has brought believers to a point where they have heard their call, then those people should be supported rather than rejected. But, so many people have been and are being rejected! What falsehood it is to bring a believer to maturity, only to deny them of the opportunity of serving the Lord in a fuller way. It's like bringing up a child but when he reaches eighteen you tell him that he can't vote, he can't move out, he can't leave the house and he can't marry or move away from home. That's not how things are supposed to be in the church. Many people have been hurt because of this type of situation. My message is this: if a person has a call on his life given to him by God, then let him walk in it or it maybe you who will be going against God's will. Remember all sin has its consequences! [Exodus 4:23].

As we move to recover things to what they should have been, there are practices that must be left behind. These are things that were allowed in the church beforehand but must now must be identified and refused access;

- Accumulating worldly treasures. We must not actively seek to acquire these things. Sure, God may bless us with them as part of our inheritance but our goal should be to build up treasure in heaven [Matthew 6:19-21]. I'll give you an example. Imagine I had a car that had been faithful to me ever since the Lord provided it for me but, I noticed that the mileage had become very high. Without consulting Him, I could make plans to go and take out a loan and replace the car. However, if I did that, where would my trust lie? Would it be in the fact that I had a new car to get me from A to B? Where should our trust always remain for our provision and salvation? In God alone [Psalm 62:1].

- Judging others. Jesus warned that if we judge, then we will be judged [Matthew 7:1]. This verse shows that even though we have been saved and God's grace has been given to us, that it does not give us the right to judge others and hold them up for scrutiny against God's standard.
- Making vows. We must no longer make empty vows (or promises) to God [Ecclesiastes 5:5-6]. If we make a vow, we are responsible for fulfilling it. We must remember that we are never able to fully comprehend God's plan for our complete lives and if we make a vow based upon our current knowledge, our future circumstances may cause us to break that vow. We cannot know what the future holds for us even if the Holy Spirit gives us glimpses from time to time. Our trust in God must always involve listening out for the next step which He wants us to take.
- Making religious ceremonies complicated. Consider this: when people in the Bible who were sick needed help, they called out to Jesus and were healed. Today we set healing into the complex structure of religious meetings. First there must be praise and worship, then a sermon and then people can come forward to receive prayer. We should be needs-focused, praying for the needs of the people and not requiring them to sit through a sermon while they are still in pain. In the New Testament we see that Jesus looked after the needs of people FIRST and then He would teach them. We need to follow the same pattern. When people went to be baptised by John or by Jesus' disciples, did they refuse them until they came back for instruction about what baptism meant? No, they didn't! People were baptised on the spot as they repented and turned to God. Another ceremony that has been made complicated is the breaking of bread. This was originally done at the start of a meal; there was no complicated religious way of doing it. Why

then should we make a huge effort to make things complicated when God wants them done in simplicity?
- Appointing people who are not appointed by God. We should not accept appointment for service from man, nor should we appoint men to hold office. God is the one who calls a person into leadership and He is the only one who can anoint them for that role. The worldly system looks at people's qualifications but God looks at the heart. We need to put more trust in God. Who would we rather trust? A person with human qualifications or a person appointed by God? Remember that God can use the unlearned to make the wise look foolish.
- Thinking building, building, building. There is no mention in the Old Testament of a building fund. Whatever they needed, they trusted God to provide. Churches do not need fundraisers; they just need prayers of faith. Also, we can become so focused on a building that we forget those who are left outside it. Do not be like those big churches which spend millions on a massive building while, at the same time, people just down the road are starving on the street. Is this the right way to show the love of Jesus, to show how He lived? He was homeless and the early church was also homeless, meeting in rented rooms, and public buildings. Interestingly, this is what made it more accessible for non-believers.

In short, we need Christ as head because, when we lead meetings by our own understanding, they usually end up in a rigid structure. We must lean on His understanding and avail of His provision. We must resist the fleshly temptation to take control of others or control of meetings and even of churches. It benefits nobody if we do such things. It would be better to just stand up and say, 'I don't know what we are doing. Let's just wait on God and see what He has to say to us: It is time for us to submit to Christ as our head.' Let us put back into our churches what it says in Proverbs:

> "Trust in the Lord with all your heart and lean not on your own understanding; in all your ways submit to him, and he will make

your paths straight. Do not be wise in your own eyes; fear the Lord and shun evil." [Proverbs 3:5-7 NIV]

We need to rid ourselves of churches that exist merely as organisations, and in their place restore the sense of family. It is more important for people to feel loved than to feel comfortable because they are a member of an organisation. We want people to know that they are accepted rather than thinking that they have to fake how they are feeling. Our aim is for real church, real family, and real people who know each other intimately. We should know the good the bad and the ugly about each other so that we can be honest with each other and help support each other through life's challenges.

We need to identify any sources of pride and cast them away from the church. There must be no boasting! The words "I'm proud of" should never be spoken by a Christian. For every thing and for every one, we should be thankful to God alone and grateful to Him for how He has created and gifted people. We need to ensure that every leader has a humble heart and; if they are not humble, then we must remove them from leadership. God opposes the proud and you do not want to have leaders who are opposed by God! Avoid telling people how good they are, how well they play music, how well they preach or how well they pray. Instead, encourage them properly by saying "God is using you or, God has His hand upon you," and so on. Finally, those who are leaders must remove their crowns (of authority) and leave them at the feet of Jesus. Many church leaders struggle with difficulties but Jesus has promised us that the yoke will be easy, the burden will be light. This easiness is not because we never carry large burdens or face big problems; it is because we can hand it over to God by admitting that we cannot take such a burden but, instead, in faith, we can leave it all at the feet of Jesus because He is faithful to answer our cry.

Chapter Five
Religion divided us
Drumcliff, County Sligo

In a very old document[4], I found something quite interesting. It was a claim that all those who come to Ireland would divide up the land. This division has been, historically speaking, one of Ireland's biggest problems. Jesus warned against division. He said,

> "If a kingdom is divided against itself, that kingdom cannot stand." [Mark 3:24 NIV]

That statement makes perfect sense. As we are at present, Ireland is divided in many different ways. There are thirty-two counties, four provinces and two nations and numerous religious groupings. I don't need to go into detail about all the troubles that have occurred in our land over the centuries. Many of us are quite well informed from what we were taught in our history classes in school and are aware that the troubles arose when English Protestant settlers ousted native Roman Catholics and took over their lands. Yet, that description of what took place is over-simplified and when you dig deeper the lines tend to become blurred. I am saying this because of the general perception of Irish history. Generations after these events, even descendants of Irish families that left Ireland still hold on to their hatred for the English. This is especially true in relation to the treatment of the Irish people during the period of the Penal Laws and the famine that began in the late 1840s. The stories and resentments have been carried down from generation to generation of how the Irish were mistreated and contributed to nationalist anti-British feelings in the 20th century.

From what I've just said, you might assume that, in order to talk about how religion has divided Ireland that I would explore the Protestant versus Catholic debate following the example of many authors and historians. However, God has revealed to me that the division in Ireland began a long time before those issues. In actual fact, I can be very specific about the particular event; it happened in the year 561. To get a greater understanding of the context, we must look at Ireland in the 6th Century in a bit more detail.

We already know that by the year 500 Christianity was already spreading quickly across Ireland. The pagan system of beliefs was on the way out because more and more people were turning to Christianity. However, during this century the seeds of division were about to be planted. Patrick had served God faithfully in northern and western regions, setting up churches in barns. Almost simultaneously, Catholic churches were spreading outwards from Leinster. It is likely that those who studied under Patrick held to what he taught, which included following the Holy Spirit. The movement coming from Leinster had originated with Palladius' mission. He had been sent by the Pope and was likely to be planting churches that followed a standardised Catholic system of belief.

At the same time as all this, elsewhere in the world there was trouble. The year 540 was the first record of the so-called plague of Justinan. This plague reached Ireland about two years later probably because of the ships coming from Gaul. We must note however that this was more than just a trade link. There was also a strong religious link between Gaul and the Leinster churches. If plague arrived by the same route as religion, then it does not take a genius to understand the spiritual significance of this. I have explained in the first chapter that religion itself is a sickness. Furthermore there were worldwide extreme weather conditions that caused crop failures resulting in famine here in Ireland and also in other parts of the world. Although this was originally attributed to volcanic activity, some scientists now conclude that it was in fact caused by comet debris called a Tunguska-like swarm throwing dust into the atmosphere and causing temperatures to drop sharply.

We can examine biblical records and see what God has to say about people who are unfaithful to Him. Let us look at the time when Ezekiel took his stand as a messenger and proclaimed what God had to say:

> "Son of man, if a country sins against me by being unfaithful and I stretch out my hand against it to cut off its food supply and send famine upon it and kill its people and their animals... Or if I bring a sword against that country and say, 'Let the sword pass throughout the land,' and I kill its people and their animals... Or if I send a plague into that land and pour out my wrath on it through bloodshed, killing its people and their animals... You will be consoled when you see their conduct and their actions, for you will know that I have done nothing in it without cause, declares the Sovereign Lord." [Ezekiel 14:13, 17, 19, 23 NIV]

So, the truth is something was going on in Ireland during that time that was bringing the judgement of God upon us. I have searched but I could not find any record as to what the people might have been doing. However, if we turn again to Ezekiel, we can use it as an example to estimate what was likely to have been happening at the time:

> "Yet in her wickedness she has rebelled against my laws and decrees more than the nations and countries around her. She has rejected my laws and has not followed my decrees. "Therefore this is what the Sovereign Lord says: You have been more unruly than the nations around you and have not followed my decrees or kept my laws. You have not even conformed to the standards of the nations around you... Because of all your detestable idols, I will do to you what I have never done before and will never do again. Therefore in your midst parents will eat

their children, and children will eat their parents. I will inflict punishment on you and will scatter all your survivors to the winds. Therefore as surely as I live, declares the Sovereign Lord, because you have defiled my sanctuary with all your vile images and detestable practices, I myself will shave you; I will not look on you with pity or spare you. A third of your people will die of the plague or perish by famine inside you; a third will fall by the sword outside your walls; and a third I will scatter to the winds and pursue with drawn sword. "Then my anger will cease and my wrath against them will subside, and I will be avenged. And when I have spent my wrath on them, they will know that I the Lord have spoken in my zeal. "I will make you a ruin and a reproach among the nations around you, in the sight of all who pass by. You will be a reproach and a taunt, a warning and an object of horror to the nations around you when I inflict punishment on you in anger and in wrath and with stinging rebuke. I the Lord have spoken. When I shoot at you with my deadly and destructive arrows of famine, I will shoot to destroy you. I will bring more and more famine upon you and cut off your supply of food. I will send famine and wild beasts against you, and they will leave you childless. Plague and bloodshed will sweep through you, and I will bring the sword against you. I the Lord have spoken." [Ezekiel 5:6-7, 9-17 NIV]

This reading highlights two things that God considers to be so detestable that it will cause Him to bring punishment upon a nation. Firstly, the people were not following what God was saying to them and instead were listening to what people from foreign countries had to say. Secondly, God always judges people who practice idolatry. In the Old Testament, idolatry was a common reason for judgement to come against a nation. Israel went into exile largely as a result of such judgement.

Many Christians feel strange having to switch their thinking from the concept of God as a loving Father to that of Him being a Righteous Judge. These are the things that cynics often jump on and cite as an example of how cruel God is, in their view. Yet, we know from biblical examples that God does bring judgement against both individuals and nations. For example, Egypt, by the miraculous display of God's sovereignty, had all of their idols and false gods challenged and torn down. Their society completely changed after that and they sent people out into the world in an attempt to discover the truth because their idols/gods had been proved to be no match for God Almighty. As Christians, we need to understand that true love also includes correction. I know that, in modern parenting, physical punishment has become somewhat frowned on, especially in today's western world. Yet we must try to understand the concept of divine correction, perhaps even by seeking revelation on it from God.

I am glad that God does correct us, but I am also glad that I have availed of His mercy. The Bible also has some great examples of men and women of God calling out to Him in intercession. Because of their prayers, God relented from His judgement. God is love and doesn't want to punish us but He will if we, as individuals or as a nation, put Him to the test. He will allow troubles to come to turn us away from an even greater disaster.

Let us return now to our discussion of Irish history. In the sixth century, monasteries started to appear in Ireland. While Patrick had supposedly attempted to set up a diocese-type system, the monastery system soon overtook everything that had been there before. The monastery and its associated theology are essentially derived from an emphasis on scripture verses such as:

> "Jesus answered, "If you want to be perfect, go, sell your possessions and give to the poor, and you will have treasure in heaven. Then come, follow me." [Matthew 19:21 NIV]

However, in Ireland, the growth of monasteries far exceeded that of Europe, and I think I can see why. Firstly, one factor would have been the influence of the famine and the plague. Naturally people were fearful and the monasteries offered them the hope of favour from God and therefore the hope of health and food. Secondly, the monastery system was also a community system and, originally, whole families could join together. Thirdly, the hierarchal system central to the monasteries resembled the old kingships of Ireland. Therefore, people settled into the structures quickly and easily because the cultural setting was so familiar to them. They worked together to grow their crops, perhaps lived a more hygienic life than the people in the towns thus saving themselves from the plague and the famine that ravaged communities elsewhere.

Spiritually speaking, it is not clear to me why judgement came on the world during these years. Perhaps one day God will reveal why these things happened. However, I do know that, due to choices made, the Irish people sank more and more into their religion. I am not inferring that it happened in this the life time of the generation of monastery planters. I say this because desperate people will inevitably call out to their creator and those who seek Him will find Him. However, succeeding generations often drift into religion if they follow the ways of their forebears, rather than retaining the understanding of why they should continually seek God.

This trend is visible if we examine Catholic historical records. Eighty-six percent of all Irish saints lived during the 5th, 6th and 7th centuries with the numbers peaking in the 6th century. Those saints who lived and died in that century represent a third of all the saints. If you include those who lived part of their lives in the 6th century, the percentage rises to an amazing fifty-one percent. This, if nothing else, helps to show how resolute the people were in these times to seek God. However, the trend did not continue after the 7th century and, the numbers of saints dropped sharply, demonstrating how the following generation had perhaps become more religious and less miraculous, or as the Bible puts it,

> "Having a form of godliness but denying its power" [2 Timothy 3:5]

By the middle of the sixth century, monasteries were being established all over Ireland. However it is important to make note that there were two separate doctrinal influences being established based on two distinct theologies. Some believers had been trained in England in such places as Candida Casa while others had been trained in Wales in such places as Mynyw. What began as a slight difference in theology would grow into a source of rivalry in the years to come.

Many of those establishing the monasteries were noteworthy people. Examples include Finnian of Clonard who famously trained the *Twelve Apostles of Ireland*; Brendan of Clonfert, Ciaran of Clonmacnois, Canice of Aghaboe, Columba of Terryglass, Brendan of Birr, Colum Cille of Durrow and Iona, Molaisse of Devenish, Ruandan of Lorrha, Mobhi of Glasnevin, Sinell of Cleenish and Ninidh of Inismacsaint. The theology of people in this group sprung from the Welsh training centres and the ideology of Gildas and both men and women in the group went on to train others. Columba of Terryglass taught Finton of Cloneagh who in turn taught Comgall of Bangor who taught the more famous Columba who wrote *Monks Rule* & his *Community Rule*.

Those who had come to establish monasteries based upon the English system were also quite famous in their time and afterwards. For example, there was Buite of Monasterboice, Coirpre of Coleraine, Finnian of Movilla, Eoghan of Ardstraw, Tighernach of Clones and Enda of the Aran Islands.

Both factions were planting and establishing monasteries across Ireland and, as a result, there were hundreds of churches and monasteries here. Yet, the places that I have listed were considered to be the most important early monastic settlements, the ones that gave Ireland the reputation as 'a land of saints and scholars'. In my research, my attention was then drawn to the life of Colum Cille who started out in Derry, then set up a monastery in Durrow, County Meath before famously travelling off to Iona and beyond. He left Ireland as if there was something that haunted him or something that had changed him. The event that affected him is on record, I believe it was the Battle of Cul Dreimhne in Cairbre DromCliabh, County Sligo during the year 561. In the previous year, two monasteries had been in contention over the ownership of a book of Psalms and this led to the battle. Colum Cille was one of the parties involved in the original dispute and it was his family that took part in the battle. He left the country soon after this event never to return.

I have to say at this juncture that, when I plotted the locations of the monasteries mentioned above on to a map of Ireland, and then revelation about the spiritual significance of what was happening came clearly to me.

On the map, you can see the locations where these monasteries were established and that there is a north-south very similar to the division that separates Northern Ireland and the Irish Republic. The battle was also fought close to the present-day border. When I saw this, I became aware that 561 was the year when the trouble between the North and South began. Its original cause was not foreigners invading the land, but religious people fighting over property. You may remember from the previous chapter how, a couple of hundred years later, the churches in the South and the churches in the North were simultaneously making petitions to the Pope in order to gain dominance in Ireland. Those in the North became the Patrican set of churches which had its centre at Armagh. Those in the South became the Columba-based churches, and their main centre was at Kildare. Columba, for example, renowned as a 'saint', wrote to the Pope to promote the mission of Palladius, saying that he alone was responsible for the church being established in Ireland. Columba does not mention Patrick at all in the letter to the Pope, because it was easier to prove the link of the Kildare based churches to Palladius. This is an example, my friend, of the extent of the rivalry that developed from the event that happened in 561.

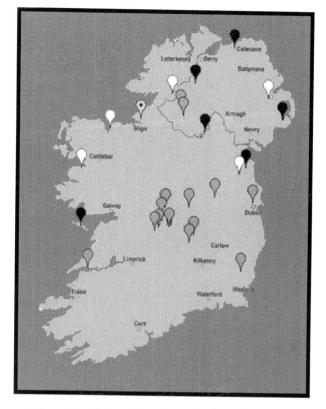

Map: church locations in Ireland in 6th century

Black = Early important monasteries of English influence
Red = Early important monasteries of Welsh influence
White = Places associated with Patrick
Yellow = Battle of Cúl Dreimhne

Religion had given birth to a divide that would grow and establish itself into what we see manifested today. Remember the words spoken over this land saying that anyone who comes to Ireland will divide up the country. Just as various conquerors came and divided up the land, religion did exactly the same. This is so much of a mind change to discover that it was not the fault of the English that Ireland is now divided. Instead, it was the fault of our own people who held on to the religiousness in their hearts and suffered the consequences.

I think that Colum Cille realised that he had been party to something terrible. His soul was laid bare. Humbled, he left Ireland as an exile, maybe because he was unable to do anything to stop what had begun. I know that he would have often prayed that, one day, Ireland would become what God has planned this precious land to be.

There is an ancient mystery which offers us that very hope. When Ireland was first established, it was divided into five Provinces or kingdoms. Today, only four Provinces remain, namely: Leinster, Connaght, Munster and Ulster but 'Cúige', the Irish word for province means 'a fifth'. One kingdom is therefore missing from our land, but it is my prayer that God's kingdom will be established here in its place. I ask God that, when my people repent and turn to Him, He will bring unity to this land, so that His name will be glorified through each of us once again. Never again do we want to see war, famine or plague in our land but when will we turn from our religious ways? The hearts of the people of Ireland have feared famine and sword, but my concern is, when will they fear God?

I want the words of the following verses to be a promise for Ireland. My desires is that we will seek God and that we will become blameless in His sight through Jesus and spend our days under God's care giving Ireland an inheritance that will endure forever. I pray that, in times of disaster, the Irish people will not falter and that, even in days of famine, our people will have plenty.

> "The blameless spend their days under the Lord's care, and their inheritance will endure forever. In times of disaster they will not wither; in days of famine they will enjoy plenty." [Psalm 37:18-19 NIV]

Having this knowledge and understanding, we made plans to travel to Drumcliff, County Sligo to the place where that battle had occurred. Two days before we were due to leave it snowed heavily but the snow melted overnight. I felt that God was speaking to me through this, that by the cutting of this religious root God was going to melt many hearts all across Ireland.

I had also realised that there are millions of Irish people, or descendants of Irish people, who don't live here in Ireland but their spiritual roots are here. I began to realise therefore that the cutting of roots here in Ireland would have the potential to reach all across the world far beyond Ireland. I am amazed by the possibilities but I don't let my mind start to think about it. Instead I want to concentrate on the task given to me.

I awoke, early one morning, with these words fresh in my mind: "Read chapters 3 and 4 of Joshua". Later, on the train to Sligo, I was resting my head on the table and I was talking with God about what He had said to me the night before, about there being twelve stones or twelve parts of this journey. It was just then that God reminded me once again to go to The Book of Joshua and to read these chapters. I opened my Bible and started to read and I was absolutely astounded by what I found. The story is of the day Joshua led the people of Israel across the River Jordan into the Promised Land. In particular, the following verses were significant:

> "So the Israelites did as Joshua commanded them. They took twelve stones from the middle of the Jordan, according to the number of the tribes of the Israelites, as the Lord had told Joshua; and they carried them over with them to their camp, where they put them down. Joshua set up the twelve stones that had been in the middle of the Jordan at the spot where the priests who carried the ark of the covenant had stood. And they are there to this day." [Joshua 4:8-9 NIV]

> "He (Joshua) said to the Israelites, "In the future when your descendants ask their parents, 'What do these stones mean?' tell them, 'Israel crossed the Jordan on dry ground.' For the Lord your God dried up the Jordan before you until you had crossed over. The Lord your God did to the Jordan what he had done to the Red Sea when he dried it up before us until we had crossed over. He did this so that all the peoples of the earth might know

> that the hand of the Lord is powerful and so that you might always fear the Lord your God." [Joshua 4:21-24 NIV]

The River Jordan separated God's people from the Promised Land. They knew something of what lay across the river; they knew it was a land of hope but also a land of challenges where they would be going to war. As the Ark of the Covenant was carried into the river, the river heaped up at a city upriver called Adam, causing the flow of the river where they stood to stop. Stones were then taken from the riverbed to remind the people of what God had done. God had opened a way through the obstacle that hindered their progress as soon as they took a step of faith and walked forward into the river. Joshua had listened to God and obeyed Him. The stones were visible proof and a constant reminder for generations to come that God had dried up the river that stood in their way. In a similar way, God was showing me that the stones we were collecting were symbolic of how He is drying up the roots of false religion in Ireland and that these dry roots will be cast into a deep sea, never to resurface again.

Furthermore, we need to understand that as soon as Israel entered the Promised Land, they were set for war. But, when the Canaanite kings heard how the River Jordan had dried up to let the Israelites through, *"their hearts melted with fear and they no longer had the courage to face the Israelites"* [Joshua 5:1 NIV]. God's enemies can fight against people but they cannot succeed in a fight against God. It was God that the enemy feared and, in turn, they also were afraid to face the Israelites because they had heard how God was with them. When the people had crossed the Jordan, they didn't immediately launch an attack or even make battle plans. Instead they came together at Gilgal to ask God to fulfil the promises that He had made to their forefathers, and circumcised themselves in obedience to God's commandments and renewed their covenant relationship with God.

> "So he raised up their sons in their place, and these were the ones Joshua circumcised. They were still uncircumcised because they had not been circumcised on the way. And after the whole

nation had been circumcised, they remained where they were in camp until they were healed. Then the Lord said to Joshua, "Today I have rolled away the reproach of Egypt from you." So the place has been called Gilgal to this day." [Joshua 5:7-9 NIV]

Gilgal was not a town but rather place which that scholars believe was a foot-shaped area symbolising Israel's claim to the land [see Deuteronomy 11:22-32]. Joshua set up the twelve stones here and the place remained a base of operations for the conquest of the Promised Land. The stones left here also were a constant reminder of their release from the enslavement of Egypt by God's power. As we read in the above passage, God had rolled away 'the reproach of Egypt' (Gilgal in Hebrew meant to 'roll'). This was also the place where they ceased to receive manna as it was no longer needed now that they were in the land 'flowing with milk and honey'. As said above, they were free from enslavement and the stones were a testimony of this fact. We too need to be free, free from the enslavement of our people by dead religion.

After we reached Sligo town, we waited for a bus to take us towards Derry, a route which went past Drumcliff. I hoped that we would be able to complete our mission and then perhaps find a cafe nearby where we could sit while waiting for the return bus to Sligo, which only operated every couple of hours! However, as soon as the bus left the outskirts of Sligo, a blizzard came down backed by high winds. We prayed and asked God to stop the snow from falling and to bring the sun out. Drumcliff was actually the first stop and we had arrived within fifteen minutes. As we got off the bus, the snow stopped and only a couple of flakes fell on us. We thanked the Lord as we walked towards the round tower. In fact in the first photograph of Drumcliff you can see the snow cloud which God had caused to move away.

The location of the monastery is now divided in half by a road, and we saw the tower on the right-hand side and the church on the left. Although the original church has long since been replaced, it is believed that it would have been located in the same place, as the door of the tower faces east. There is also a high cross in-between the tower and church.

Photos: Tower with snow cloud (top left), high cross (top right) and round tower with a cleared sky (bottom)

We walked around the church grounds and discovered that this is the place where W. B. Yeats was buried. Indeed, there was a little craft shop there which specialised in selling things associated with him, such as bookmarks with his poems. It was a nice shop but I couldn't help but feel that the place was maintained as a pilgrimage site in memory of the man. It seemed to us that the place was celebrated more because of

Yeats than because of Colum Cille who had lived there and set up a monastery in this beautiful location. I couldn't help but try to think what it would have been like to live in such a beautiful place. We prayed and declared aloud everything that God had been speaking to us about, saying quite specifically that the root of what began in this area in the year 561 would dry up (just as the Jordan dried up when the priests stepped into it in faith).

As we waited for the bus, the sun came out and shone down upon us. Surely this was an answer to our earlier prayer, and confirmation to us that God was hearing all our prayers and answering them. I am confident, therefore, that all of the roots of division in Ireland will now unravel because we saw how God was with us, and saw His purpose in this mission. I also have to mention that as soon as we got back into the train station, the wind and the snow returned. We watched the deteriorating weather from the safety of the station and were really thankful to the Lord God for helping us to avoid any severe weather at Drumcliff.

Chapter Six
A time for reconciliation

We are instructed by Jesus [Mark3:24] that a kingdom cannot survive if it is divided against itself. Yet if we look at the modern Christian church, an organisation that is supposed to be extending the kingdom of God on earth, we see that it is very much divided. In fact, at present, there are somewhere in the region of 41,000 Christian denominations across the world. In chapter three I explained how the number of denominations increases. They increase as a result of one person or more, realising that something isn't right in their church/denomination so they then leave and start a new church/denomination. The problem about this is that a kingdom must not be divided against itself. This means that the current Christian church as a whole cannot be considered to be a united kingdom. If we are not extending God's kingdom but rather spreading division, then something in us has to change. Paul made an appeal about division in the church when he wrote to the Corinthian believers:

> "I appeal to you, brothers and sisters, in the name of our Lord Jesus Christ, that all of you agree with one another in what you say and that there be no divisions among you, but that you be perfectly united in mind and thought. My brothers and sisters, some from Chloe's household have informed me that there are quarrels among you. What I mean is this: One of you says, "I

follow Paul"; another, "I follow Apollos"; another, "I follow Cephas "; still another, "I follow Christ." Is Christ divided? Was Paul crucified for you? Were you baptized in the name of Paul? I thank God that I did not baptise any of you except Crispus and Gaius, so no one can say that you were baptized in my name. (Yes, I also baptized the household of Stephanas; beyond that, I don't remember if I baptized anyone else.) For Christ did not send me to baptize, but to preach the gospel—not with wisdom and eloquence, lest the cross of Christ be emptied of its power." [1 Corinthians 1:10-17 NIV]

We can see that from the start, there were quarrels in the church among the believers. From the above verses we see that the believers in Corinth were fighting over who was greater based upon who had originally trained them. Remember how the claim of superiority leads people down the wrong path. These believers were obviously basing their significance on who they followed in order to prove that one group was better than another. Yet here we see Paul state clearly that any preaching by him carried out in wisdom and elegance would empty the cross of Jesus of its power! Here is why. The message of the cross is a declaration that without Jesus we are lost. It focuses on Him whereas preaching in one's own strength takes away from the sufficiency of what God has done through Jesus. It makes us proud and boastful. Along with this, if we are boasting in a teacher whom we follow, we reduce our testimony of Jesus and lose the opportunity to boast in Him alone.

Quarrels like those in Corinth have always existed. Even in Ireland you can easily see the divisions, both in religion and culture, that are largely based on which ideology or theological persuasion has been followed. Even in the modern evangelical churches there are great divisions. When I studied psychology, one of the areas that we covered was prejudice. What most people don't know is that prejudice is a natural inclination of the mind. I researched how teenagers form groups that have particular identities. These teenagers focus on what is good about their own group while pointing out the things they don't like about the other groups. Each group adopts its own social identity, what its members do, where they go, what they wear, what music they listen to and so on. It is this type of mentality that psychologists use to explain the origin of prejudice, racism and even genocide. This similar to what happens in and between our churches. We point at what we do right and point out what others do wrong. We join a church, follow a pastor, whom we may raise up above other pastors. Doing so, we see seeing our particular church as preferable and somehow we remain unable to understand why everyone doesn't attend it!

As soon as we assign a church denominational status, or just a name, we run the risk of causing division. This is because people will tend to create a culture within that church system according to what they believe, what they do, what kind of music they sing to, what they wear, when they meet for worship and so on. Then maybe they will tend to look down on other churches, or even the churches that they have come from, in order to highlight the good things about their own church. But there is no division in the true church of Jesus Christ, it is His Body. So if division exists between particular churches or denominations, or even between individuals, then we might begin to suspect that they are not really part of the true church. But it is not quite as simple as that. The true church of Jesus Christ is not defined by a building or a pastor or a theological position. Instead, it is defined by the hearts of individual believers. Indeed, the true church overcomes all religious rulings and cultural or socio-economic distinctions. Each true follower of Christ, therefore, is an integral part of the church of God; it is something that each of them has in common. This is what Paul makes clear to the Corinthians:

> "Just as a body, though one, has many parts, but all its many parts form one body, so it is with Christ. For we were all baptised by one Spirit so as to form one body—whether Jews or Gentiles, slave or free—and we were all given the one Spirit to drink. Even so the body is not made up of one part but of many." [1 Corinthians 12:12-14 NIV]

Therefore, for example, a person in Mexico who is a believer and follows Jesus is part of the same church as I am. I may never have met him, I may not know him but through Christ we are brothers and will share heaven together. Should I then build up a partition wall and say, "No wait! He is a Catholic. He can't be my brother," or "He is a Baptist and so he can't be my brother". If a person is a true Christian, such divisions are destructive and contrary to the Word of God. If we are led by the Holy Spirit, he will bring us into perfect unity with our fellow believers. But religiousness will always counter the work of the Holy Spirit by inserting man-made ideas and doctrines that cause division between one believer and another.

> "But avoid foolish controversies and genealogies and arguments and quarrels about the law, because these are unprofitable and useless. Warn a divisive person once, and then warn them a second time. After that, have nothing to do with them. You may be sure that such people are warped and sinful; they are self-condemned." [Titus 3:9-11 NIV]

This verse speaks very powerfully against the causes of division. It says here to warn a divisive person or, as it puts it in another translation, warn the person who stirs up division. Here it is stated that division comes from people quarrelling and having disputes over the law. This, Paul wrote, is what that has divided people and divided churches.

The problem is that when such divisions or church-splits occur, they will leave hurts and confusion in the hearts of the believers that may last for many years. We must not accept such outcomes any longer. There will always be disagreements in the church but this is only because our understanding of God is not yet complete, nor will it be until the day we meet Him in heaven and all truth is revealed. Therefore, disputes stem from the fact that two or more people do not yet understand God's truth on that subject and hold to what they know and argue their case rather than seeking God for answers. Remember, there is no believer who has a complete grasp of God, at the very best, we are only seeing God through dark glass. A person might have 10% or 60% or even 99%

but never 100%. This is why each one of us must individually reach maturity so that we are not dependent on other believers who have an imperfect theology. We need to be totally dependent on God for a perfect theology in order to meet the various situations that arise in our lives.

It would be wise to pause here and take a moment to consider what idolatry is. From our understanding of the Bible, we normally view idolatry as bowing down in worship to stone or wooden idols that represent various deities. Although, what is seen here is wrong, what really matters to God is what is going on in the hearts of the people. God wants our devotion and, if we love him, He will be the focus of our worship. Idolatry, therefore, is the worship of anything that draws our attention away from God. Yes, people can worship metal or wooden idols but people can also worship possessions or other people. They could idolise a football star, a winning team, a TV or film character, a video game or a variety of other things. Sadly idolatry can also happen in the church. The congregation might idolise a church leader or a worship leader. Idolatry always brings swift judgement from God and that can happen with a church too. God is love and is always seeking to correct us when we turn away from him. However, we must take care not to defile the sanctuary with any form of idolatry such as vile images or detestable practices. I also include here the removing of any element of money-making from the church. There should be no book-sales or CD sales. We should always remember what Jesus did when He found people buying and selling in the Temple! He said that His house should be a house of prayer and not a profiteering 'den of thieves'. I am not saying that there shouldn't be resources provided but we should always make those resources available free of charge.

The reason why I introduced the subject of idolatry is that, in some cases, God may have sent someone to challenge a church leader on some issue or other. There always has to be a place for accountability and correction, even for church leaders. When we fall away from doing what's right, we need correction and must love God's corrective measures, no matter how they come to us. It is a good thing if we love being disciplined.

> "Whoever loves discipline loves knowledge, but whoever hates correction is stupid." [Proverbs 12:1 NIV]

In many cases, where people have tried to correct a leader, ended up in a lot of trouble. Out of resentment, they might be ostracised or perhaps even asked to leave the church. But that situation arises when, the leader assumes that he knows better. Quite often, he is supported by a group of believers who have put their trust in their leader instead of those who are seeking God for the truth. If a person has had to step forward to correct a leader, then it is always a possibility that God had no choice but to send an 'outsider' in order to deliver whatever message the leader had been refusing to listen to. Their sin, when challenged in front of a congregation can bring to the surface human reactions of denial and self-protection but, the truth remains, God knows the hearts of everyone, and there is no hiding from Him. There is the real danger that where pride of position gathered from people's admiration, festers and becomes idolatrous, that disaster will follow. Pride comes before a fall.

Removing the person who spoke out will not make things right! Others who heard them speak may ponder their doubts about the issue and perhaps leave later on. However, the person who has been removed will not have been dealt with in a loving and fair manner and the person who needed to repent and turn to God will have ended up in 'a deeper hole' than at the beginning. Therefore, the only way to resolve such situations is for everyone to keep an open mind, and then come together to seek God for direction and for the truth. Only then will everyone be dealt with fairly and with love.

> "Be completely humble and gentle; be patient, bearing with one another in love. Make every effort to keep the unity of the Spirit through the bond of peace." [Ephesians 4:2-3 NIV]

There is a very important thing to learn about division: division causes people to be exiled!

In December 2013, I left the church that I had been attending and, certainly, for quite a while I felt like an exile after the way that I had been treated. But I am thankful to God that He has brought a full healing to my heart. Recently, He has begun to speak to me about the people that I had left behind. When I left, I didn't tell anyone except the leadership. At the time I felt this was the right thing to do as I did not want to be accused of stirring up division. Nevertheless, division still occurred. Friendships and mentorships were torn apart and it was a struggle. But I have not closed my heart to the matter because I know that reconciliation has to and will come. There may be people there who were hurt because I did not confide in them. There may have also been others who were confused about why I left. But God has instructed me that, as part of this journey, that He wants me to begin to be reconciled with the people who were left behind. That process has already begun, and I trust God to bring about full reconciliation, even if it takes years. Yes sometimes, it does take years, especially if one side has closed their minds. In that case, reconciliation may not happen until the day when we all reach heaven. Nevertheless, we must make every effort, as Paul wrote. It is vital that we have harmony so we can keep building each other up.

> "Let us therefore make every effort to do what leads to peace and to mutual edification." [Romans 14:19 NIV]

It can be a difficult thing to be reconciled to others. This is because it means that both parties have to admit fault. Indeed, whilst I know that it was right for me to leave the church, perhaps it was not done with the right attitude or using the right words. I have to accept the fact that, by me following God, others can get hurt in the process and unfortunately, that is the way of how it is when you step out in faith. However, God does not want us to hold on to feelings of anger, judgement or disappointment and so we must be willing to make every effort to be reconciled with anyone hurt by our actions, even if they were done with the best of intentions.

> "Be kind and compassionate to one another, forgiving each other, just as in Christ God forgave you." [Ephesians 4:32 NIV]
>
> "Whoever claims to love God yet hates a brother or sister is a liar. For whoever does not love their brother and sister, whom they have seen, cannot love God, whom they have not seen." [1 John 4:20 NIV]

The problem of course is that church has been seen more as an organisation than as a family. I will talk about this in more detail in a later chapter. In the ancient church, people were excommunicated for the smallest of errors without recourse to the proper way of correcting a brother as set out in Matthew 18:15-22. That kind of thinking is flawed. Do you imagine that God would divide up heaven, for example, by putting Baptists in one room and Pentecostals in another in case the Baptists hear the Pentecostals speaking in tongues and start debating their theology? We are all one family and we will all share the same heaven one day. Therefore, we must learn to get along in the knowledge that when we reach heaven we will know the full Truth and our individual theologies won't matter anymore.

Doggedly supporting a religious divide such as a denominational distinctive issue name only serves to reinforce the walls between you and others. In Irish history, we have seen how division manifested itself and grew into something much bigger with divisive issues continuing through the centuries. Will you be content to see that situation continuing on into the future?

You see, the devil simply does not fear a divided church because a divided church has no power to overthrow what he is doing! But if we are united in the singular purpose of seeing God's will being done, then the enemy will have to flee before us. At a meeting last year, a brother shared a prophecy that had been spoken over West Dublin several years ago: "The Spirit of God is here but He hovers way above, waiting for unity between believers". Such unity cannot be achieved through human reasoning or human systems. Neither can it be achieved by getting all parties to agree to basic theological statements that they find agreement on. The focus must always be on obedience to God, and to reach the lost and lead those new believers into a mature relationship with God. Mature believers do what God says. There is no need to argue over theology. The Bible says, that doing so is 'unprofitable and useless'. Indeed, what expansion has ever happened in the Kingdom of God through arguments over theology? None. On the other hand, consider the expansion that occurs when people listen to God and obey His will.

Here are a few simple statements that we all must accept:

- I will not have one-hundred percent truth until I reach heaven,
- My primary responsibility is to mature as a believer and do what God tells me,
- I am in no position to judge any other person because I am still flawed,
- If I love God, then I must love all my brothers and sisters despite their flaws. For the sake of peace, I have to overlook their flaws and not talk about them behind their backs. Instead, I must protect them, even if it means laying down my life for them,
- If any brother or sister needs correction, then it must be done in love, carried out in the way Jesus taught us,
- We should never force people to become exiles,
- We should make every effort to be reconciled with those whom we may have fallen out because of theological debates or through leaving a church or through a church split,
- We must celebrate Jesus alone as the one who established and is building our church,
- We must never evaluate anyone or anything higher than Jesus.

Most of all, we need the Holy Spirit who can melt our hearts and remove any root of bitterness that is lingering there. Jesus gave a wonderful promise that those whom He sets free will be free indeed.

Chapter Seven
Religion gave our inheritance to the enemy
Rock of Cashel, County Tipperary

Do you remember the verse that God gave me during the first part of this journey, specifically these lines?

> "The voices of testimony are born vibrant but are wasted away
> Because religion does not produce an ongoing testimony."

This is what I believe began to happen to the monasteries as they continued after the 7th century. Two centuries before this there had been miraculous signs and wonders but now the number of mighty men and women of God was dwindling. As time went on, the rules in the monasteries increased making them more and more strict. As this happened, it began to prevent the Holy Spirit. Eventually, all that was left were the monasteries and their religious way of life. However, living in a religious environment does not produce people with an active testimony of Jesus. So too today, when people become engrossed in the week-to-week running of their 'church', they can lose their testimony. As a replacement for it, they focus on what their 'church' is doing or, perhaps, in the 7th century, what their monastery was doing. They talk about the things that brought their church into existence, the mighty things that have already happened and the great events that they have planned for the future. Yet, in reality, they have a humdrum existence with pre-planned programmes setting out times for prayer and fasting, times for work, times for the study of the Word and times for various events. Everything is pre-set: set songs, set verses and set behaviour patterns. Everything is set to order by man-made rules that are made to satisfy human standards and human traditions.

When you live like this, an introverted cultural system is created that does not easily relate to people in the outside world. Newcomers may be seen as people who have to come on board to be trained into the system. Sometimes they just don't fit in and so they wander away or, worse still, are asked to leave. The end result of this will be no-one going out into the world anymore. The whole church will become inward looking and have people who are focused in on themselves and others in the group who are with them. Their thoughts might become like this: "I need to learn more before I am ready," or, "I need to pray more" or "I need to study more." They are focused, therefore, on what they feel they need to mend in their lives and in their minds before they can take action. Also they calculate what scholarly qualifications they would need to have before they could even think about sharing the Word of God with anybody. What qualifications or training did the twelve disciples have? None. They were simply willing to follow Jesus. They became baptised with fire as they were filled with the Holy Spirit. Patrick carried this fire in his life, he wrote saying, "God ordained me, God sent me". As for the modern Irish church, where has that fire gone?

Figuratively speaking, the monasteries put their heads into the sand. They concentrated more upon rules and regulations and, by doing so, failed to live the truly penitent existence that they reached for. The Bible speaks clearly about those living a self-styled penitent life that is born out of rules and regulations:

> "Such regulations indeed have an appearance of wisdom, with their self-imposed worship, their false humility and their harsh

treatment of the body, but they lack any value in restraining sensual indulgence." [Colossians 2:23 NIV]

In modern times, some people are locked into this kind of system that has its roots going right back to the time of the monasteries. While they may mean well, their hearts merely seek the completion of programmed weekly events rather than developing a love-fuelled relationship with God. When their programme is complete, they feel complete. In the Bible, Jesus spoke about people who have got their priorities wrong:

> "These people honour me with their lips, but their hearts are far from me. They worship me in vain; their teachings are merely human rules." [Matthew 15:8-9 NIV]

As mentioned previously, since about the year 795, the Vikings came to Ireland and attacked monasteries throughout the country. God surely allowed this to happen in the hope that the Irish people, especially those who had become rich and powerful might turn from their religiousness and seek His ways. Later on, the Norsemen settled here and intermarried with the Irish, and some even fought battles together with the Irish. In the 11th century, Brian Boru fought alongside the Norsemen to become the first High King of Ireland. However, three years later in 1014, he was killed at the Battle of Clontarf but his victory signalled the defeat of the Norsemen in Ireland. Everything was being set in place for dramatic change!

I believe that as Catholics in Ireland entered the 12th century, things had become so stale for them that they recognised the need for change. The same kind of situation has arisen today. Many of us have come to realise that church as we know it is not working. Yet, as said in chapter three, there is a cycle of religion that people get trapped in. Remember how, after someone realises that something is wrong with their church, they chose to start afresh but take a piece of their religion with them. This is exactly what happened for all the monasteries at this point in time in Ireland. It was a turning point for the Irish people, a golden opportunity had come to us to turn to God and shed our religious ways.

Would the Irish people follow God or go deeper into their religion?

Unfortunately, so-called 'wise' men decided what was wrong was the lack of proper structure in the Irish Church. As they looked across at the continent, they saw that the Catholics there had long since left behind the monastic type of settlements and, instead, had opted for churches to be built and organised into dioceses that were governed by bishops. Furthermore, they could see that a diocese had already been set up in Dublin by the Archbishop of Canterbury. So a decision was made to convene a synod in order to discuss the matter. In fact, four synods in relation to the issue took place during the 12th century. At the second of these, in the year 1111, a decision was made that they would replace the old abbey system with the diocesan system. This change was possibly instigated by a man named Maolmure O'Dunan but there is some doubt about him. However, some records show that he was given the land of Cashel, County Tipperary in 1101. Indeed this was where the first synod took place during that same year. The significance of this is that Cashel, previously known as 'The City of Kings', now lay in the hands of the Irish church. I believe that the church leaders made immediate plans to use this new seat of power and that this led to the following synods. Their initial plans excluded Dublin but it was added later.

Maolmure died in 1117 but others carried on with his ideas. 'Saint' Malachy was one of those who took up the cause. Malachy was one of few Irish saints of the 12th century. He had worked his way up in the church until, in 1129, he had gained the position of Archbishop of Armagh and Primate of Ireland. Part of his work included taking those plans for the diocesan structure to the Pope in order to gain his permission for the changes. This would not have been an easy journey and, despite travelling all the way to Rome on his first attempt in 1139, the plans were rejected. He then undertook to make a second journey in 1148 with plans of an amended structure but he died on way. Between these two journeys Malachy established the very first Cistercian house at Mellifont. This Cistercian system was an even more austere one than what had been there before and included, for example, the making of vows of silence.

Eventually, the amended diocesan plans which Malachy had tried to deliver to Rome, reached there at the hands of another person, and was approved. The Pope sent one of his cardinals, Paparo, to Ireland to finalise the matter. It took Paparo two attempts to reach Ireland but, when he finally made it, the diocesan system was established in the year 1152. Once again, the land of Ireland was carved up, this time into even smaller sections than before. Spiritually, the ownership of Ireland had shifted and something devastating was about to happen. With papal permission, in 1169, the Normans, along with Diarmuid 'traitor King of Ireland', arrived at Bannow to invade the country. This was followed by another army which was led by King Henry II of England. He landed in 1171 near Wexford at Loch Garmen. Below is a summary, showing the sequence of events during this period:

1101: The 'City of Kings' was handed over to the Irish Church. The first of four synods occurs.

1111: At the second synod, The Irish Church decides to install a diocesan system.

1111-1148: The church in Ireland seeks papal approval for the intended changes.

1152: Dairmuid betrays Ireland to King Henry II and Cardinal Paparo arrives in Ireland to officially approve the diocesan system.

1155: The (English) Pope gives permission to the Normans to invade Ireland.

1169:   The Normans invade Ireland

1171:   King Diarmuid dies. Strongbow, an Englishman takes his place and

King Henry II lands with an army to ensure Strongbow's continued allegiance to the crown.

1172:   King Henry II demands a fourth synod and compels the Irish church to submit to the English church.

The most shocking thing here to learn from this is that the Pope, an authoritative figure to whom the Irish church had just submitted was the person who gave permission for the first major Anglo-Norman invasion. I believe that the claim that Ireland belongs to England has its roots in this point of our history. Our own religious and political leaders, who sought to achieve importance and power by means of greed, inadvertently handed control of our land over to foreigners. We would suffer the aftermath of these invasions for over 700 years!

Despite the invasion by Henry II, the diocesan system still went ahead. Soon new churches were being built to replace previous structures and continued to be built across Ireland during the years 1171 - 1348. A lot of these were simply built on top of the church buildings that had existed previously. As Edith and I travelled to ancient sites during our journey, we had to recognise that most of the ruins were of churches built during this period of history.

What historians tell us is that the Pope's motives probably were two-fold. Firstly, he believed that the Irish church was too independent. Secondly, he wanted tithe money coming in from Ireland. The financial deal struck with the Norman king was a payment of one penny per hearth per annum. Later in the 16th century, this selfish and greedy decision would haunt the Catholic Church (when the English King, Henry VIII, converted to being a Protestant). But I think that we will leave that story for now and come back to it later in our journey.

It is worthwhile to note at this point the role of Diarmuid Mac Murchada who had been a king here in Ireland. He was deposed from the throne and had to flee the country because of animosity due to his despicable behaviour. He promptly went to King Henry II, in the year 1152, and swore an oath of allegiance in return for an army with which he could seize back his kingdom. The Anglo-Normans, hungry for land, immediately took the opportunity to gain more territory and, after permission was granted by the Pope, an army under the leadership of Strongbow was despatched. However, Diarmuid died in 1171 soon after the invasion and this is why King Henry II came over to Ireland with another army. It was to ensure that Strongbow would stay loyal to him. It was not a co-incidence in 1152, the same year that the Irish diocese was approved, that our land was betrayed by Diarmuid. He, of course, thought he would regain his kingdom but, instead, he allowed power and authority of his rule to fall into the hands of the Anglo-Normans. The Irish had previously surrendered their spiritual rights to the land of Ireland and, because of that, they lost their physical rights to sovereignty. Every action has its consequences and the consequences here cost us our freedom.

I firmly believe that if we had turned from our human way of thinking and sought God at this point in our history then God would never have allowed the Normans to come here and, the 700 years of strife that came afterwards may never have happened. Once again, my forefathers and fellow Irishmen did not make the right decisions but turned away from God. It is possible that they may not have realised their mistake. Back then, the Pope was seen as the ultimate authority but today we know from scripture that Jesus is the head of the church. With hindsight, it is easy to look back at those people and point accusingly at them. However, I will say it again, our mission is not to attack people but to recognise the errors made by them and intercede in prayer with God for our land and for our people that we would learn from the past and be open for God to bring us into a brighter future.

We find these words in Matthew's Gospel:

> "For there is nothing hidden that will not be disclosed, and nothing concealed that will not be known or brought out into the open." [Matthew 8:17 NIV]

The first of the four synods had been held in Cashel, the 'City of the Kings' but the last synod also took place there too. It was held in 1172 after the invasion at the request of King Henry II, and it was at this point that the Irish church had to submit to the English church and became answerable to it as regards rules and finances. A few years later, in 1203 a new system of tithes was introduced into the diocesan system. The greed had originated in Cashel in 1101 but now, just over 70 years later, the possibility of financial reward was stripped away from them. The greed had brought its punishment. Remember, greed is a form of idolatry and practicing idolatry brings the judgement of God upon any person or land. It wasn't just the fact that the church was stripped of some of its finances, the whole country had to suffer as a result of those decisions. Then in 1311, an eight-year famine struck Ireland. How sad, that once again, because our people had behaved in such a way that brought the judgement of God upon them.

I knew that I would have to make a journey to Cashel in order to pray there but the place was a bit out-of-the-way for me. For some reason, I had thought that I might come to work in Limerick at my employer's head office (as I do periodically) and from Limerick, Cashel would be closer. When I checked, I realised that it would still require adding on quite a bit of distance to go via Cashel on my way back to Dublin. Also, if I was working in Limerick, then I would be there for a full day and would not be able to gain access to the castle at Cashel at all. I did not have a solution to this dilemma but I knew that God would work it out for me. And He did.

A couple of days later, I got a call from my in-line manager in Limerick and he asked me to train a new member of staff how to clear debit-notes. This person worked in Ballyragget, in County Kilkenny. My boss added that if I went, I could be there for ten and finish at two. Not only was Ballyragget a lot closer to Cashel but I would have time to spend there and the company would be giving me enough money to cover my petrol costs. What a fantastic answer to prayer! Don't imagine for a moment that it is normal for me to go to Ballyragget. Actually, I had never been there before and, while I normally go places to teach Health and Safety, I had never been asked to teach someone how to clear debit-notes. It was a miraculous answer to prayer and I was filled with joy when it happened.

The down-side was that I was going to have to do the trip alone as Edith would not be able to go with me to work. Instead she would be backing me up with prayer and fasting as I undertook the journey. For some reason I decided that I would go to Cashel on my way to Ballyragget. So I got up and left home really early so that I would have around 45 minutes at the site. I had never been to Cashel before and so I had a little 'wow-moment' when I first saw it, soon after coming off the motorway. It looked huge even from a distance. I drove into the town and found a car park but it required payment. I decided not to park in there because I didn't have enough change. Also it was deserted and if the machine weren't working then I might get stuck in there! I saw a couple of vans parked nearby on double-yellow lines so I pulled in behind them and asked the drivers to kindly keep an eye on the car for me for a few minutes.

Photos: Rock of Cashel (left) and the valley below (right)

From there, I walked up the hill to see if I could get inside the site. Unfortunately, but there was no way to get inside; I would have to wait until it opened at nine o'clock. I made a swift calculation and realised that I would only have about 15 minutes inside before I would have to leave for Ballyragget. I returned to my car and moved to another street where there was free parking. I walked back up and climbed on to the side of the hill and began to pray. I repented for the mistakes that had been made there in the past and prayed as the Holy Spirit led me. As I prayed and asked God for verses relevant to what happened at this location, God gave me this scripture from Ezekiel, and I saw a parallel between what God said about Israel and what He was showing me about Ireland:

> "Son of man, these men have set up idols in their hearts and put wicked stumbling blocks before their faces. Should I let them inquire of me at all? Therefore speak to them and tell them, 'This is what the Sovereign Lord says: When any of the Israelites (Irish people) set up idols in their hearts and put a wicked stumbling block before their faces and then go to a prophet, I the Lord will answer them myself in keeping with their great idolatry. I will do this to recapture the hearts of the people of Israel (Ireland), who have all deserted me for their idols.'
> "Therefore say to the people of Israel (Ireland), 'This is what the Sovereign Lord says: Repent! Turn from your idols and renounce all your detestable practices! " 'When any of the Israelites (Irish people) or any foreigner residing in Ireland Israel separate themselves from me and set up idols in their hearts and put a wicked stumbling block before their faces and then go to a prophet to inquire of me, I the Lord will answer them myself. I will set my face against them and make them an example and a byword. I will remove them from my people. Then you will know that I am the Lord. "'And if the prophet is enticed to utter a prophecy, I the Lord have enticed that prophet, and I will stretch out my hand against him and destroy him from among my people of Israel (Ireland). They will bear their guilt—the

prophet will be as guilty as the one who consults him. Then the people of Israel (Ireland) will no longer stray from me, nor will they defile themselves anymore with all their sins. They will be my people, and I will be their God, declares the Sovereign Lord.' " [Ezekiel 14:3-11 NIV]

At this point, Edith sent me verses that God had led her too while praying. They had to do with people turning away from their first love and becoming a people who were self-seeking.

"Love is patient, love is kind. It does not envy, it does not boast, it is not proud. It does not dishonour others, it is not self-seeking, it is not easily angered, it keeps no record of wrongs." [1 Corinthians 13:4-5 NIV]

"Yet I hold this against you: You have forsaken the love you had at first. Consider how far you have fallen! Repent and do the things you did at first. If you do not repent, I will come to you and remove your lampstand from its place." [Revelation 2:4-5 NIV]

I read all these scriptures out loud and then prayed and interceded and declared that the time of judgement for idolatry will come to an end and that we, the people of Ireland, will return to our first love, that we will be His people, and that He will be our God. Then, as I knew my time was limited and that the castle would probably not be busy on this cold winter's day, I prayed that I would be able to get admission, that the staff would not delay in opening up and that I would receive their favour. My prayer was answered. I got admission on time and and they did not even charge me the full entry fee. Praise God!

Photos: cathedral at Rock of Cashel (left) and cornerstone (right)

In the two photos above, you can see something that very much interested me. On the left, you can see where part of the cathedral wall has collapsed, and there on the ground lies a huge stone, a cornerstone. This cornerstone is not small in size but would in fact be much bigger than a man. You can estimate the size of it if you compare it against the size of the doorway. For me, this was confirmation of the verses that Edith had sent me. It illustrated the truth that the people here had lost touch with their first love and that Jesus, who is the chief cornerstone, had been removed from His rightful place. I prayed and declared that Irish people will no longer keep Jesus from being the first love in their lives but instead give Him pre-eminence over everything else.

Also of interest to me at Cashel was Cormac's chapel. This had been named after the king of Munster, Cormac Mac Carthaig and was the building with scaffolding around it. They were not intending to restore it but were attempting to protect the stonework from rainwater. Inside the chapel, I found a wonderful room that had originally been beautifully decorated but now only sections of those paintings remain intact. According to records, the round tower on the site was built first, around the year 1100 and it is believed that this chapel was built soon afterwards, between 1127 and 1134 and that carpenters had been sent from Germany to assist with the building. This means that the building was in place when King Henry II came to Cashel to address the synod of

Ireland. Perhaps I was standing in the very room in which that meeting took place.

Photos: Cormac's chapel

Also significant and worth a mention is Hore Abbey which sits in the valley just below the Rock of Cashel. It was given to the Cistercians in 1270. If you remember, the Cistercian movement in Ireland was first established at Mellifont by Malachy. However, Hore Abbey was the last

Cistercian establishment before the monasteries in Ireland were dissolved. Malachy was linked to the synods held at Cashel. I believe that it was here that he first had the idea of establishing Mellifont. Why? Because, as I have noticed while on this prayer mission that where something begins, it quite often ends. This was certainly true, for example, with the sin of greed committed at Cashel coming to completion when King Henry II arrived to take away their wealth and power.

Chapter Eight
Take it all back!

In order to get into position for claiming back our inheritance, we must first understand what our inheritance is and then how we might go about recovering it. To start off, let us think for a moment about this statement:

Self-imposed worship is done in vain

This simple statement is a combined summary of Colossians 2:23 & Matthew 15:8-9 which were quoted in the previous chapter. 'Self-imposed' means something you require of yourself, something that you expect yourself to be doing. It is not done because of what someone else has said. 'Vain' means to have a very high opinion of something which has produced no result. Putting this all together and you could say this:

Self-imposed worship is a time of worship you that impose on yourself,
It is an event, or events over a period of time which you regard as being important
but, in reality, it produces no results.

What am I referring to? In essence, I am referring to events in the church. I think the time has come when we must seriously consider how we do church because, in my view, churches have become primarily event-focused and this is reflected by the social networks which are frequently used by churches advertising their events and their special speakers. Sadly, it is often the case that, when special speakers are visiting churches there is a higher attendance than usual.

The thing is that we are all called to walk with God and that is our greatest inheritance. It is made possible for us as believers. It is what Adam experienced before the fall. Imagine walking with the Almighty, the One who created everything! This is our greatest inheritance for sure, and in the end times, it will be our destiny to live like this [Revelations 21:3]. Walking with God, therefore, is not a three-event-a-week routine but a lifestyle, a life-choice to live every hour of every day in His will. If we have boxed God in and compartmentalised Him then we are not walking in our inheritance but, instead, we are merely being religious. When God first challenged me on this topic, I wrote the following paragraphs [15]:

> So we move to the last side of the box. This is the top of the box and it is connected to each of the other four sides and it represents tradition. We touched on this a little when talking about worship, how humans love to have routine, and how routine gives us a sense of safety in an uncertain world. I remember, for example, when my daughter was little. People would often offer me advice and one thing that a lot of people said was, 'Get her into a routine early.' We did that and she responded well. So, even from childhood, routine suits us.
>
> In each of the following four areas we get into a routine. With money we pay regular bills or have regular spending habits. For example, routine involves the type of food we buy and where we buy it. It affects where we park in the parking space when we go shopping. We will even drive along a certain route to the shops or when going to work or to the bank. The thing is, when we do these things just because it's what we always did, we can miss what God wants us to do. Remember the challenge given us in the Book of Proverbs: **"In all your ways acknowledge him,**

and he will make your paths straight" Prov 3:6. Perhaps God wanted you to go to a different shop than your usual one so that you could meet an old friend and have an opportunity to witness to him or her about God. If we don't know maybe it's because we never asked. Maybe we were so stuck in our routine of how we do things that we were unable to respond.

The same thing applies to time. We develop routines. We say, "This is when I go to bed", "This is when I go to church", "This is when I take a shower" and "This is when I will read my Bible". Building up traditions like these is not good. What if God suddenly wanted you to pray for a friend on holiday who has just been in a serious accident and He wakes you up in the middle of the night to pray for that person? If you are stuck in your routine, you might reply, "Oh no God, not right now, I need my sleep." Do you not think that if God gives you an instruction to do something, will He not also give you the energy to complete that task? Remember what Paul wrote in his epistle to the Philippians: **"I can do everything through him who gives me strength" Phil 4:13**. *Therefore let us be aware of your routine so that we can always be listening to hear from God and be willing to break from your routine.*

We must also be aware of routine and tradition in the area of prayer. Imagine if you were getting to know someone romantically and he or she assigned you certain times of the week when you were allowed to visit or make contact. You would soon be so frustrated with their behaviour that you would probably stop seeing them. How do you think God feels when you define and specify a routine time for you to talk with Him? If you don't do that with your friends or family, then why do it with God?

Similarly, when we have our worship time, we must be careful not to get into a routine of what songs or which method we use in worship. Each worship time should be unique and special and each time can be if we let it! I believe that there are levels of freedom in worship that we have not even begun to explore. I am excited by this idea that we can push on into the unexplored. Imagine for a moment, something such as a 24-hour worship session made up of only spontaneous songs composed on the spot! There is nothing stopping us from such things except ourselves and the routine we have made.

So, as routine and tradition come together in these different ways, they complete the box. Inside this box is where we keep God. It is not intentional that we do these things but yet we do them and keep God boxed up. Then, we wonder why God is not moving powerfully in our lives. The answer is simple. He is not moving powerfully in our lives because we are stopping Him from having unlimited access to our hearts and lives. When we do that, we struggle against God instead of submitting to Him and His authority. This is contrary to the counsel given in James' epistle: **"Submit yourselves, then, to God. Resist the devil, and he will flee from you"** *James 4:7. The good news is that there is a solution. We can turn to God for help to break away from the things that hold us back from reaching our full potential. What will happen then? We will get back to seeking a deeper relationship with God that will ignite a hunger that only He can satisfy. In fact, only this will keep us moving forward on our journey with God* [Extract from Be Revived: Open the Box[15]]

As I have mentioned elsewhere in this book, our prime focus should be to listen to God and to obey Him. Yet many of us end up instead obeying the events that we and others have created. How many of us read or study our Bibles on a Sunday afternoon? Do we think that just because we had 'church' in the morning we don't need to think about God again that day? What if we attend an event when God wants us to be somewhere else? If that were the case, then we have sinned. Yet in our minds we believe that we are acting correctly.

Here is another simple statement for us to consider:

Time spent at events is often spent in vain.

For me, this is hard to accept. How do we know if something has been done in vain? Should our answer be based on how good the music was? Should it be based on what was preached or taught? No, the measure by which we need to go by is fruit. An example of this might be how we worship. In my book *In Spirit and Truth*[14], I explained in detail how God measures our worship. I made it clear that, if we have not been changed during our worship then we have not really been worshipping at all. Instead we may have been just singing songs. How many of us have done that in our lives? How many of us are still doing it? In order to walk with God, listen and talk to Him you must have an active participation in the worship. However, at the kind of events that we often attend, we may not be actively participating with God but rather participating with the event. I'll give you two examples:

- **Example 1:** The worship music has started and you start singing along with the lyrics on the screen. God, however, at that moment maybe wants you to pray and ask for forgiveness. However, you ignore that prompt from the Holy Spirit and carry on singing songs. At the end, the worship is so powerful you feel blessed by it. Then you happily take your seat and wait for the preacher to speak.
- **Example 2:** The worship has started, and you immediately go deeply into worship but then God gives you a word for the whole church to encourage them. Instead of saying anything, you wait through the whole service but no opportunity to speak arises. This means that everybody goes home without hearing that word of encouragement from the Lord that He gave you to share.

There are several other examples of this and I am sure that you could think of a few too. When we come to have fellowship together, our focus must be on seeking God, and not mere compliance with the format of a particular event. There needs to be huge flexibility because Jesus as the Living Word is likely to speak to people during the worship and those people should be allowed to share what He is saying. The biggest argument against this, and I will only mention it here for those who are doubters, is the 14th chapter of 1st Corinthians. If these verses are understood in a certain way, it can be interpreted as 'worship time must be structured'. Yes, we do need orderly worship, but by whose order? Our first priority is to be obedient to Christ, therefore we should go by the order that God gives us. Actually, I see this particular chapter in Corinthians as not being written in an attempt to bring human order but rather to get rid of it. It shows how a Holy Spirit-led meeting can run smoothly if people have respect for each other and listen to each other. It says that all are not to speak at the same time, nor should all prophesy at the same time. It even says that if one person is speaking but another gets a revelation from God, then the first person should stop speaking in order for the church to hear what the other has to say. How challenging is that! Why have I never seen such a thing happen in any church that I have been to? It is probably because such things cannot happen within a structured event. And no one is immune from arranging such events, not even men.

Last year, for example, Edith and I began a fellowship group. Our hope was that we would create a free space set apart for God to work through us in a spontaneous way. Some of the meetings were fantastic. We received prophecies and visions and unbelievable answer to prayer, even healings right there on the spot. At first, I was really pleased about the times when we gathered and I still believe that there were many prayers said then that will continue to be answered over the coming years. However, after about six months, I became aware that something was seriously wrong, a piece was missing. Each of us had learned to worship freely with no set songs but with spontaneous song choices and on-the-spot song writing. We had also learned to pray with freedom, not restricted to one-at-a-time but with several people calling out simultaneously to God in an unstructured way. What was missing was the fact that it had become an event, held at a set time every week when in reality, what God wanted was that we would seek Him at any time of the day or night. For us, we were unable to operate at this level at the time because we were renting a room and so we had to have a set start and finish time. I long for fully spontaneous fellowship and I know that God will allow such things in the future, because He wants to walk and talk with us on a daily basis.

When we look back into Irish history, we can see the point at which the Christian community realised that change must happen. We are at that point once again. We have to make a choice but there are two options. The first is to look at what other people are doing in other places and copy their formats. Then we can organise an ever-increasing amount of events and ministries that are perceived as greater both by name and by reputation. The second option is to turn to God and listen to what He is telling us to do with our churches, as He calls us to leave vain events and, in their place, seek both a passionate relationship and passion-filled time with Him.

In Irish history saw how, when authorities seized our inheritance, they divided up the wealth and only gave a portion of it back. This makes me question what happens in our modern churches. Do the church leaders in effect divide up the full inheritance that we should all share? That inheritance is our daily walk with God, in a passionate relationship. Are we handed out God's blessing in dribs and drabs, like scraps from the table, just little snippets of information? Maybe, on our own part, we don't go seeking God enough and are content to sit back and not aim for the highest. Perhaps our leaders don't understand that the full inheritance is there for us all and not just for a certain elite. There are no elites in God's kingdom, there is just God and us. There is no one who has the right to exercise spiritual authority over us except God. We are adopted as full adult members of the family of God. We are a royal priesthood. There is no lack in our inheritance, just a lack of people who are claiming it! Paul spoke about this when he wrote to the believers in Galatia:

> "What I am saying is that as long as an heir is underage, he is no different from a slave, although he owns the whole estate. The heir is subject to guardians and trustees until the time set by his

father. So also, when we were underage, we were in slavery under the elemental spiritual forces of the world. But when the set time had fully come, God sent his Son, born of a woman, born under the law, to redeem those under the law, that we might receive adoption to sonship. Because you are his sons, God sent the Spirit of his Son into our hearts, the Spirit who calls out, "Abba, Father." So you are no longer a slave, but God's child; and since you are his child, God has made you also an heir." [Galatians 4:1-7 NIV]

When we walk in our inheritance, we have God with us every moment of the day and what is produced by living such a life increases that inheritance. You simply have to ask and things are given to you. Where there seems to be no way to move forward, God even goes before you to make a way. You experience miracles and see prayers being answered right before your very eyes. You see the impossible become reality. That kind of life produces a living testimony. Instead of preaching or teaching people, you can begin to share your story of how Jesus is actively revealing Himself on a daily basis to conquer any enemy or overcome any difficulty. God's glory is magnified by people living this kind of life as He is honoured and no one else. In the New Testament at the very start of the church, people just shared the experiences they had had with Jesus and told how He had met with them and what He had said to them or done for them. Today, people who behave like them are rare. The testimony frequently heard from people these days tells how they prayed once several years before and God saved them. Sadly their active testimony has never developed or has been suppressed by the consuming effects of belonging to a religious system. I believe that the time has come to restore the active testimony of what Jesus is doing for us today!

When we walk daily with God our focus will change. Over the years churches, and the events that they organise, have become very inwardly focused but, when we walk in an active relationship with God, we become much more outwardly focused. This happens because we come to love God so much that we yearn for Him and request to hear what is on His heart. Then He shares with us the secrets of His heart, such as how He feels about the lost. When God reveals His heart to a person, they are changed forever. Its impact is so much more than any sermon can make. I remember listening to a teaching by David Wilkerson, when he spoke about anguish[18]. He was speaking in a very challenging way about the lack of people today who are anguished over the things they see happening around them. At that time I sought God and asked Him specifically about worship. When He revealed His heart to me, it changed me forever. I could never go back now to how I used to lead worship in my youth. In fact, I had to repent on account of how I led worship in my youth! We can hear things from other people but, when God shows us something, it is absolutely life-changing.

When we become outwardly focused, then we begin to care about things that we let slip by us before, such as the importance of making friends with people who don't know God. It's a total change of mindset. It puts detail into our prayers. We start to pray, for example, for drivers who act carelessly on the road ahead of us asking God that they may get home safely, rather than complaining about them like we used to do. We stop to feed or give money to the needy instead of walking past them as if they didn't exist. When we hear about people being sick, we pray for them to be healed, rather than just passing on our regards to them. All of us must come to the point where we live a godly life if we want to inherit the land of promise that God has for us. Our hearts won't be revived by attending meetings or by having extra music practices or from hearing visiting speakers. We will have revival through seeking God, finding Him, obeying Him and walking with Him. It is simple, but that does not necessarily mean that it will be easy. There is always a cost. We are called to give up our lives, to give up our selfish ambitions, to give up any pride-of-life, in fact, to give up absolutely everything. We must also be willing to give up everything that we will ever receive in the future.

When we look back at the events of history, we can see how people removed Jesus from being their focus time and time again. They removed their spiritual cornerstone and suffered the consequences.

The benefit of history is that we can learn from the mistakes of our forefathers and countrymen and choose not to repeat them. We must accept absolutely nothing less than a full inheritance. We must seek God until we have achieved that inheritance, and that will take us a lifetime. Let us not be fooled into thinking that by being more religious we can reach God. In fact, the more religious that we become, the further away from God we will get. Where will that leave us? The truth is, we chose wrongly in the past. We made wrong decisions. We can either change now or choose to walk forever in that wrong way, the path where God is kept at a distance from our hearts.

Our ancestors chose to be more religious, and ignored the commands of God who was telling them to keep a hold of their inheritance. As a result, we lost it all. We lost the inheritance of Irish sovereignty for hundreds of years. Just as it was in the physical, so it was in the spiritual realm. Immediately afterwards, famine arrived in Ireland. Famine is what faces us if we sacrifice our inheritance. We put ourselves into a state that leaves us with only the bare scrapings of an existence, starving ourselves at spiritually-dry events. We will talk in more detail later on about the concept of 'spiritual famine'.

Our ancestors mistakenly thought they were acting wisely by taking man-made ideas and applying them to Ireland when God had a very different plan. As a nation we leaned on our own understanding and not upon the wisdom and guidance of God. Is a priest God? Is a pastor God? Is a pope God? None of them are. Who knows the will of God? Only those who humbly seek Him will ever understand the mysteries of His person. Humble people always put others first but, most importantly, they put God first. Will God reveal His heart to a man with pride in his heart? No. Will God reveal His heart to a man who is selfish and self-seeking? No. Why then should we seek wisdom from such people and expect them to be able to tell us God's will? Do not be deceived by false humility! If a person stands up in a meeting and tells people how humble he is, is he really humble? If a man stands up and boasts of doing great exploits, exploits that he has done for the Lord, is he humble? We must forget our idols and detestable practices and seek

God!

Therefore, let us not settle for spiritual poverty but press forward to gain the unfathomable riches that God has in store for us. Let us catch a glimpse of those 'riches' as we read the following scripture verses:

> "The righteous will inherit the land and dwell in it forever." [Psalm 37:29 NIV]

> "I will proclaim the Lord's decree: He said to me, "You are my son; today I have become your father. Ask me, and I will make the nations your inheritance, the ends of the earth your possession." [Psalm 2:7-8 NIV]

> "Be strong and courageous, because you will lead these people to inherit the land I swore to their ancestors to give them." [Joshua 1:6 NIV]

> "See, I have given you this land. Go in and take possession of the land the Lord swore he would give to your fathers—to Abraham, Isaac and Jacob—and to their descendants after them." [Deuteronomy 1:8 NIV]

Perhaps you have just woken up to the fact that our inheritance has been taken away from us. That being the case, let us see how God led David to reclaim what had been taken away from him:

> "When David and his men reached Ziklag, they found it destroyed by fire and their wives and sons and daughters taken captive. So David and his men wept aloud until they had no strength left to weep. David's two wives had been captured—Ahinoam of Jezreel and Abigail, the widow of Nabal of Carmel. David was greatly distressed because the men were talking of stoning him; each one was bitter in spirit because of his sons and daughters. But David found strength in the Lord his God." [1 Samuel 30:3-6 NIV]

What this passage shows us is that our inheritance includes our children. This is something which I talk about in more detail in a later chapter, to show how our children were stolen in the past and how they are still being taken from us today. At this point David had a choice. Let us try to put ourselves in his position. The easiest response to the situation would be to go and try to take back our inheritance using our own strength. David could have done that. His men were with him, greatly distressed and probably even calling out for vengeance. In fact they were so angry and bitter that they almost stoned David. But David did not give in. In the face of impending mutiny, he found strength in the Lord his God. He then made a decision to seek the Lord God for instruction as to what to do next:

> "Then David said to Abiathar the priest, the son of Ahimelek, "Bring me the ephod." Abiathar brought it to him, and David inquired of the Lord, "Shall I pursue this raiding party? Will I overtake them?" "Pursue them," he answered. "You will certainly overtake them and succeed in the rescue." [1 Samuel 30:7-8 NIV]

Now, consider for a moment the significance of David asking for the ephod. In Exodus, the ephod is described as a garment that the high priests wore underneath the breastplate. Let us connect that fact with a New Testament verse concerning a breastplate, that is called the breastplate of righteousness [Ephesians 6:14]. Righteousness reflects God's holy standards and means doing what is morally right. What David was essentially doing was seeking God's will to find out if it was morally right for him to pursue the people who had taken his inheritance. Why did he do that? I believe there were two reasons. Firstly, he knew that it is God who allows our inheritance to be taken from us. This might have happened because of pride or idolatry, which God detests, or for some other reason. From this story we learn that our first step is to get right with God and then ask God to help us get back our inheritance. Secondly, David wanted to make sure that the recovery of his inheritance would be done by God's strength, not by his own efforts. We will see the results as we follow the story:

> "David and the six hundred men with him came to the Besor Valley, where some stayed behind. Two hundred of them were too exhausted to cross the valley, but David and the other four hundred continued the pursuit. They found an Egyptian in a field and brought him to David. They gave him water to drink and food to eat— part of a cake of pressed figs and two cakes of raisins. He ate and was revived, for he had not eaten any food or drunk any water for three days and three nights. David asked him, "Who do you belong to? Where do you come from?" He said, "I am an Egyptian, the slave of an Amalekite. My master abandoned me when I became ill three days ago. We raided the Negev of the Kerethites, some territory belonging to Judah and the Negev of Caleb. And we burned Ziklag." David asked him, "Can you lead me down to this raiding party?" He answered, "Swear to me before God that you will not kill me or hand me over to my master, and I will take you down to them." He led David down, and there they were, scattered over the countryside, eating, drinking and revelling because of the great amount of plunder they had taken from the land of the Philistines and from Judah." [1 Samuel 30:8-16 NIV]

David could not possibly have organised it so that an Egyptian would be found who would betray his masters and lead David and his men to where they needed to go. This is the kind of thing that happens when God's strength is at work in a situation. As He promised, He goes before us to make a way. We learn from this that God wants us to reclaim our inheritance and if we seek Him and are willing to trust Him fully, we can get it all back just as David did:

> "David fought them from dusk until the evening of the next day, and none of them got away, except four hundred young men who rode off on camels and fled. David recovered everything the Amalekites had taken, including his two wives. Nothing was missing: young or old, boy or girl, plunder or anything else they had taken. David brought everything back. He took all the flocks and herds, and his men drove them ahead of the other

livestock, saying, "This is David's plunder." [1 Samuel 30:17-20 NIV]

Not only did David get back every part of what had been taken from him, he also recovered what the raiders had taken from other people as the Amalekites had raided more places than just Ziglag. In fact he claimed back an abundance of stolen goods. Yet because he was aware that he had only won it back by God's strength and not his own, he did not lay claim to the plunder. He was not greedy with it. He saw that by sharing it equally with others the glory and honour would be given to God:

> "Then David came to the two hundred men who had been too exhausted to follow him and who were left behind at the Besor Valley. They came out to meet David and the men with him. As David and his men approached, he asked them how they were. But all the evil men and troublemakers among David's followers said, "Because they did not go out with us, we will not share with them the plunder we recovered. However, each man may take his wife and children and go." David replied, "No, my brothers, you must not do that with what the Lord has given us. He has protected us and delivered into our hands the raiding party that came against us. Who will listen to what you say? The share of the man who stayed with the supplies is to be the same as that of him who went down to the battle. All will share alike." David made this a statute and ordinance for Israel from that day to this. When David reached Ziklag, he sent some of the plunder to the elders of Judah, who were his friends, saying, "Here is a gift for you from the plunder of the Lord's enemies." David sent it to those who were in Bethel, Ramoth Negev and Jattir; to those in Aroer, Siphmoth, Eshtemoa and Rakal; to those in the towns of the Jerahmeelites and the Kenites; to those in Hormah, Bor Ashan, Athak and Hebron; and to those in all the other places where he and his men had roamed." [1 Samuel 30:21-31 NIV]

Just as David did, we must seek the Lord and ask Him to help us take back our inheritance. This is what I did at the start of this journey. I wanted Ireland to regain its full inheritance and, as you have read, at every place we visited, we found that God had gone before us to prepare the way for us. I am confident, therefore, that God will restore the inheritance of Ireland and even give us more than what was taken from us. As individuals we must all do the same. We must rid ourselves of our wrong thinking and allow God to guide us into the future He has planned for us, and recover our inheritance. That is my hope for you, because it is God's purpose for you. I want to be able to walk through my land of Ireland and look to my right and to my left and see people enjoying the fullness of their inheritance. The question is, will you be one of them? I pray that you will.

Chapter Nine
Religion led us to rebel
Clonmacnoise, County Offaly
St Marys Abbey, Dublin

If you remember, I said previously that when Ireland was put under the rule of the English by papal authority this would come back around to haunt the Pope. I believe that this happened because God truly loved Ireland and its people. Just as we as a nation have had to face the consequences of our actions, so did other nations and I think that God brought punishment on the Vatican for the decisions made there that led to the Anglo-Norman invasion and subsequent settlements. I believe that it was at least part of the reason why God spoke to people like Martin Luther and John Calvin about the errors in Catholic doctrine. Their challenge resulted in the so-called Protestant reformation which is normally accepted as having run from 1517 to 1648. However, in truth, it started long before 1517. The Moravian church, which is the oldest Protestant church, was actually founded in 1467, decades after its forerunner stood up to the Vatican. This church dates back to a man called Jan Hus who taught a doctrine of justification by faith alone. He was summoned to the Council of Constance and, refusing to recant, was burned at the stake as a heretic in 1415. The Moravian church survived this persecution but eventually its members fled to Germany where they found sanctuary with Count Zinzendorf in the town of Herrnhut.

Over the years, several good things came out of people being set free from Catholic domination. One example was the missionary movement which had its origin with the Moravian missionaries coming from Herrnhut. This movement spread the Gospel all over the world. Ireland was affected by the Protestant Reformation after King Henry VIII left the Catholic Church and declared himself as head of the Church of England on 11th February 1531. Although his decision was most likely based on domestic reasons, it introduced dramatic changes to the English Church. However, the Irish Church, which had been put in submission to the English Church chose to remain Catholic. Henry never went so far as to enforce religious change in Ireland.

I believe that there was a golden opportunity here for the Irish People. We had endured hundreds of years of political oppression because of religious choices made by the pope. In 1531, the opportunity arose to let go of the religion that had sold Ireland out to England. It was a chance to renounce man-made religion which had brought so much trouble on the country. Although the Church of England was to remain closer to Catholic Church doctrine than the Protestant movement had done at the start, Ireland could have used the opportunity to completely shrug off Rome's influence forever. Instead, filled with resentment towards what they saw as their foreign oppressors, they viewed the Protestant movement as rebellion against papal authority. They gave in to public opinion rather than fighting together against an enemy that had oppressed them since the days of Palladius. Once again, what God was saying to the Irish people was ignored. Jesus wanted them to follow Him [Matthew 4:19], but instead they chose to follow the teachings of the pope in Rome.

I believe that this act of refusal activated several spiritual issues for the people of Ireland. For this part of our journey, we are going to look at the subject of war and rebellion. In the curse pronounced by God in Deuteronomy chapter 28 we find this portion of scripture:

> "The Lord will bring a nation against you from far away, from

the ends of the earth, like an eagle swooping down, a nation whose language you will not understand, a fierce-looking nation without respect for the old or pity for the young. They will devour the young of your livestock and the crops of your land until you are destroyed. They will leave you no grain, new wine or olive oil, nor any calves of your herds or lambs of your flocks until you are ruined. They will lay siege to all the cities throughout your land until the high fortified walls in which you trust fall down. They will besiege all the cities throughout the land the Lord your God is giving you. Because of the suffering your enemy will inflict on you during the siege, you will eat the fruit of the womb, the flesh of the sons and daughters the Lord your God has given you. Even the most gentle and sensitive man among you will have no compassion on his own brother or the wife he loves or his surviving children, and he will not give to one of them any of the flesh of his children that he is eating. It will be all he has left because of the suffering your enemy will inflict on you during the siege of all your cities. The most gentle and sensitive woman among you—so sensitive and gentle that she would not venture to touch the ground with the sole of her foot—will begrudge the husband she loves and her own son or daughter the afterbirth from her womb and the children she bears. For in her dire need she intends to eat them secretly because of the suffering your enemy will inflict on you during the siege of your cities." [Deuteronomy 28: 49-57 NIV]

In 1641 a rebellion broke out in Ulster. It began with attacks on settlers who had come during the English Plantation and then intensified. It would become known as the eleven year war. Many of the English were forced out of their homes even though it was in the middle of winter. In places such as Portadown, Armagh and Tyrone thousands of people were killed with many killed in incidents that were recorded as massacres. The actual number of people killed is unknown but it could be anywhere between 12,000 and 200,000. The latter figure was used later by the English Parliament in order to gain support for an invasion of Ireland. As the conflict continued, massacres continued to occur on both sides, especially after troops landed in Ulster from Scotland to support the Plantations. Although the rebellion may have had its roots in the frustration of those who had had their land seized from them and given to others, it soon gained political and religious significance.

I want to focus in particular on religious developments at the time. Two meetings were held in March 1642 and both of them were attended by members of the Catholic gentry and the church hierarchy and at both meetings, support was voiced for the war as being a 'just cause'. These two meetings were held in the towns of in Trim and Kells in County Meath. In May of that year, the Irish Catholic Confederation was formed and a parliament was established in Kilkenny City, making Kilkenny the capital of Ireland in preference to Dublin. No longer was Dublin the capital of Ireland, but Kilkenny. The oath that was taken by all those involved had been produced jointly by a bishop and a lawyer and included a declaration of allegiance to Charles I, the deposed Catholic King of England, and a call to arms to fight for religious freedom for Irish Catholics. The wording of the oath that was taken is very important in the context of what we are discussing here. Of particular significance is this sentence; "I will, during my life, bear true faith and allegiance to my Sovereign Lord, Charles".

The word 'sovereign' means a supreme ruler or monarch but it also means a person possessing supreme power. There should be only one Sovereign Lord in our lives and that person is Jesus Christ. Yes, we are instructed in scripture to submit to authorities, which means, for example to comply with the laws of the land [Romans 13:1] and to pay our taxes [Romans 13:6] but this does not contradict the truth that God is above them, above everything, is God. He is the supreme authority and our belief in that truth is essential for our salvation.

> "If you declare with your mouth, "Jesus is Lord," and believe in your heart that God raised him from the dead, you will be saved." [Romans 10:9 NIV]

As we know, salvation is not just about getting a ticket for heaven after we die. It is also a salvation that we experience everyday of our lives, being totally dependent on God to keep us. What we see happening was that an oath was taken accepting Charles I as sovereign, and by doing so, people put their trust in him for their salvation. However, our only hope of salvation is through Jesus Christ. There is no other one and no other way.

In a situation where a government treats us with cruelty or perhaps brings in laws that are contrary to Christian belief, or even persecutes us by prison or sword, we ask, "Is it right to rebel?" Two things must be considered. Firstly, that it is God who has allowed the government to rule over us and so, to rebel against them, is to rebel against God. Secondly, it is a promise in scripture that those who do wrong will be punished and so, these authorities are not bringing a 'sword' without reason [Romans13:4]. To raise arms and fight against corrupt rulers is never God's way. Understanding this principle has taken away the feelings of disgust that I had at what the English did here in Ireland. You see, our salvation is not found by exerting our own strength through rebellion or through depending on the strength of others, such as priests, bishops, or others in positions of authority. Our salvation depends only on Jesus Christ. If we submit to Him, obey Him and act righteously in a time of persecution, then we will discover Him as our strength. We need to remember that if God has put a corrupt government in authority over us, then, to change our situation, we must seek God and repent of our wrongdoings. His promise is to hear from heaven and save us. In the same way that He sets up rulers to rule over us, He can remove them from power and change the season that we are going through. Daniel certainly knew the truth of this and depended on God's intervention time and again during his exile in Babylon:

> "He changes times and seasons; he deposes kings and raises up others. He gives wisdom to the wise and knowledge to the discerning." [Daniel 2:21 NIV]

What happens when we rebel against the people who rule over us? Let us go back to the example that we were looking at. A religious and political rebellion, against the English but also against God began with massacres across the plantations but it was doomed to failure from the start. Who are we to rebel against God? Rebellion against God always results in disaster. The decision to rebel was instrumental in shaping future events in Ireland. The English were stirred by desires both for justice and revenge and Oliver Cromwell, incensed by stories of how people in the plantations had been massacred, decided to come to Ireland to force the rebels into submission.

In 1649, on hearing that Cromwell was about to arrive, the rebels made plans to take Dublin so that he would not have a port to land in. However, they suffered defeat due to a surprise counterattack on the 2nd August when thousands of Irish men were either killed or taken captive. Cromwell arrived with 35 ships full of troops on the 15th August followed by another 77 ships two days later. Remember the application of the verse in Deuteronomy 28 which stated that, under God's curse, our cities, the places which we trust for protection would be put to siege and then taken. That is exactly what happened! The ferocity of Cromwell's forces left an indelible mark on the memories of the Irish. When rebels refused to surrender, they we were massacred. Whole towns were captured and burned. Thousands of soldiers and townspeople were either killed or taken captive and crops were so severely destroyed that famine spread. Cromwell and his soldiers were repaying us in full for the massacre of the people in the plantations. The following is a list of some of the major battles against Irish towns and cities:

- The Siege of Drogheda (3rd – 11th September 1649)
- The Siege of Wexford (2nd – 11th October 1649)
- The Siege of Kilkenny (22nd – 27th March 1650)
- The Siege of Clonmel (April-May 1650)
- The Sieges of Waterford (Nov-Dec 1649 and June-August 1650)
- The Siege of Duncannon (1650)
- The Siege of Limerick (June-October 1651)
- The Siege of Galway (Aug 1651-May 1652)

A couple of weeks before entering this part of my journey, I was watching a live broadcast from *Glory of Zion* where a lady was sharing about how she had discovered something in her bloodline that was important for the anointing that God had put on her life. In her case, God was calling her to be an intercessor for Israel. What that lady shared left quite an impression on my heart. As I sought to find out more from God about my life, I began to notice how certain dates in my life matched dates referred to in my description of this journey.

My family name is Harper, a name which seems to have originated in Scotland. The name probably comes from someone who played the harp and so was called a 'harper'. One thing I discovered as I thought about this is that, biblically speaking, there is something very interesting about the harp. The original Israeli harp was called the Nevel harp and had 22 strings. The significance of this is that there were 22 letters in the Hebrew alphabet and so the Word of God could be expressed musically using a harp. King David was a harp player and I began to wonder if the Psalms can be played using the music of a harp just as they were originally played by David, playing each Psalm word by word. Although I don't play the harp, I did actually learn the basics of playing it as a teenager and even learnt to strum one song. My family name must count for something after all!

The information about the harp gave me a lot of insight into music, even making me rethink the whole subject altogether! Furthermore, I recalled that when King Henry VIII made himself King of Ireland in 1531, the harpers of Ireland were so famous that the harp was adopted as the symbol of Ireland. This began with the harp being stamped on to new Irish coinage that was being produced at that time.

As mentioned above the Harper name probably originated in Scotland. I know that my father has records showing that my more recent ancestors came from County Fermanagh. This is interesting as Fermanagh was the location of one of the Ulster plantations that occurred in the period 1610 to 1630. It is a possibility, therefore, that this was when my ancestors first came to Ireland, along with those

Scottish plantation settlers of Fermanagh. If this is the case, it would also mean that my family were survivors of the attacks by rebels in 1641. However, on checking the Munster Rolls[8] a document that lists the family names of Plantation settlers in Ulster, I found that the name 'Harper' only appears once and refers to a man in County Donegal called John Harper who had rented land from Sir James Cunningham. His land was in an area known as Portlough.

I could find no definite link there to my family name but, however, there was already a link to the Cromwell era that I did know about. When Cromwell was on his way to put Kilkenny under siege, word was sent to a garrison at Cantwell's castle which was located four miles northeast of Kilkenny requesting assistance. Instead of supporting Kilkenny city, as some of the soldiers based at the castle were English, they decided to support Cromwell instead. I found this fascinating as the ruins of this very castle came to be owned by my grandfather during the 1940's. The original Cantwell family had come after the Norman invasion of Ireland but, during the rebellion period, Thomas Cantwell of Cantwellscourt had become fully dedicated to the Confederate cause and was referred to by others as 'a cruel and bloody rebel'. In 1653, his son John, had the estate confiscated from him and the family fled to Connaught. There are records indicating that some of the Cantwells found their occupation in the church. Oliver Cantwell, for example, was the Bishop of Ossory from 1487 to 1527, one of the 24 dioceses set up in 1152. Another Cantwell who found his occupation in the church, was called Fr. Joannes Cantwell. He was present when the Synod of the church was held at Clonmacnoise in 1649. This was a very significant event that helps us to understand our history.

Twenty-one archbishops, bishops and other clergy gathered at Clonmacnoise for the Synod, a meeting that lasted ten days. By this time, Clonmacnoise was no longer a working monastery and had fallen into disrepair. It is likely that they chose the location to gain some spiritual significance or authority. After the Synod they published a statement which would have been read out in every parish. I acquired a copy of this document, along with Cromwell's response to what they were declaring. The document appealed to Irish Catholics from all over the country, asking them to forgive each other of any differences in the past and to unite as one body in order to fight against Cromwell and the English. They said this despite acknowledging that it was God who had allowed Cromwell to come, and despite admitting that the invasion was "God's wrath fallen on this Nation"[7]. They went on to state categorically that no one should accept terms from Cromwell, take either his religion or his money, but join together in unity. If they didn't, they would be punished. They wanted to fight "in hope that by the blessings of God they may be released from the threatened evils"[7]. However, Cromwell also knew that he had come to Ireland because God had allowed it. In his response to the Synod he wrote, "Is God, will God be with you? I am confident He will not"[7]. He evens goes on to condemn the Archbishops, the bishops and the prelates for encouraging the Irish to engage in a bloody war, stating that this would cause them 'confusion' and saying they had led the Irish into a 'ruinous heap'. The Catholic hierarchy, therefore, were fully aware that they were inciting rebellion against what God had allowed, and so did Cromwell. This is how the Irish people were set up to lose the war by their own religious leaders.

The rebellion of 1641 was very significant for the reasons I have mentioned already and probably was Ireland's most successful rebellion. However it wasn't the first rebellion that had occurred in Ireland against the English, nor would it be the last! The very first rebellion took place in 1534 when Thomas Fitzgerald heard a rumour that his father (the Lord Deputy) had been executed in London by King Henry VIII because of support given by the House of Kildare for the Pope in opposition to Henry. As an act of defiance Thomas went into Saint Mary's Abbey and threw down his Sword of State. Then, with a band of followers, he attempted to take Dublin Castle but failed terribly in spite of having some cannon guns at his disposal. This rebellion was born out of a son's love for his father and anger at those who had supposedly killed him. But this first rebellion led to many more rebellions, all of which, according to Romans 13, can be considered to be evidence of rebellion against God. Here is a list of the major Irish rebellions that took place from 1534 to 1883:

1534, 1569-73 & 1579-83	The Fitzgerald rebellions
1641-1652	The Irish Catholic Confederation rebellion
1799-1803	The Society of United Irishmen rebellion
1848	The Young Ireland rebellion
1867-85	The Fenian Brotherhood rebellion
1882-83	The Irish Nationals' Invincibles' rebellion

List of Irish rebellions before The War of Independence

So, in order to undo the spiritual roots of how religion led us to rebel against God, I knew that we had to go to the two relevant locations of importance: Saint Mary's Abbey in Dublin, the birth place of rebellion, and to Clonmacnoise. We went to these places to repent for those who actively chose to rebel against God using religion as their motivation.

There is something of spiritual importance here that I still do not fully understand. It is about how my family came to own some of the land of the Cantwells, the very family who had been stripped of their land because of support for the Confederate cause and for the Synod of Clonmacnoise. With the possibility of my family having been among the Plantation settlers attacked during the rebellion, I realised that God has surely watched over my family in that they ended up owning some of the land belonging to the people who rebelled against God. This is challenging. Perhaps it is as it is so that I can repent on their behalf. Maybe God's power can enable you to repent for those who have attacked, or even killed your family.

Our journey continues. As it happened, I was due to go to Limerick on either a Friday or a Monday morning to attend licence renewal training for my job. A colleague got first choice and so I ended up knowing that I would travel on Monday 2nd of March. As part of the trip, I planned to visit Clonmacnoise the same day. I knew that it would add on an hour to my journey time plus some more time for prayer so I reckoned that I might be able to travel there before work, just as I did when I visited the

Rock of Cashel. That morning, I woke before dawn and got myself ready only to discover as I opened the door to leave that it was snowing. I have to say that I panicked a little as there was no way to know what the roads would be like between Dublin and Clonmacnoise. I prayed and waited. However, when it came to the time when I had to leave, the snow still hadn't stopped so I made a decision to cancel going to Clonmacnoise that morning but to trust God to make a way for me to get there in the afternoon. I set out for Limerick.

When I left home and got beyond our housing estate, I found that the roads were not as bad as I had feared, but when I got to County Tipperary, the snow returned and, as the motorway there didn't seem to have been salted, so the driving suddenly became quite treacherous. I slowed down. Then I saw a car just ahead of me go off the road. It didn't crash but the driver had to swerve because the person in front of him had jammed on his brakes. Later on, I discovered that this was one of the men who would be attending the training with me. As I got nearer to Limerick the roads improved again and I arrived at the office safely but a little late. I began to question God, "Why did you make it snow today?" I couldn't understand why He would do that, knowing that I needed to get to Clonmacnoise. Was it a test of faith? Was it a test of strength?

When the training began, the trainer told us that because we had travelled from all over the country and because the weather was so bad, he was going to do things differently and try to get finished as early as possible. The man was true to his word and, by two in the afternoon, I found myself sitting in my car ready to set out for Clonmacnoise. The snow had cleared from the ground by this stage but it had begun to snow again. However I was confident and even more so because one of the other trainees had passed near Clonmacnoise that morning and had told me that the roads there were not too bad. I had all I needed, information about the local roads and the extra time to visit the site. I wouldn't have had this extra time if I had gone to Limerick and it hadn't snowed! In that case I would have been there until perhaps four or five o'clock. How amazing is God that He caused the whole day to turn out as it did!

I had to take a lot of back roads to get from Limerick up to Clonmacnoise but amazingly they were all clear of ice and snow and, as I neared the location, the sun even came out to greet me. I felt blessed as I pulled into the car park, knowing that God was watching over me. For some reason I had envisaged Clonmacnoise to be easily accessible in a field but, instead, it was closed off and I could only get in via the Visitor Centre. I could see immediately that, if I had left for Clonmacnoise early that morning, I would not have been able to gain entry! I thanked God that He had guided me so that my mission could be completed.

Photo: the two towers at Clonmacnoise

As I walked around the site, I read out Bible verses that Edith had sent to me:

> "Surely then you will find delight in the Almighty and will lift up your face to God. You will pray to him, and he will hear you, and you will fulfil your vows. What you decide on will be done, and light will shine on your ways." [Job 22: 26-28]

As I read this, I felt great encouragement because the day that I had just experienced seemed to prove that 'light will shine on your ways'. I also prayed that the Irish people would delight in God and that they would pray to him. I prayed that He would hear them and that they would fulfil their vows to God. My hope was that God would stand with us and make things happen as they should. The Holy Spirit reminded me of these words from the time of Solomon's building of the temple:

> "The Lord said to him: "I have heard the prayer and plea you have made before me; I have consecrated this temple, which you have built, by putting my Name there forever. My eyes and my heart will always be there. "As for you, if you walk before me faithfully with integrity of heart and uprightness, as David your father did, and do all I command and observe my decrees and laws, I will establish your royal throne over Israel forever, as I promised David your father when I said, 'You shall never fail to have a successor on the throne of Israel.'" [1 Kings 9:3-5]

In another version it states that God would establish a throne for Israel forever. As I read this, I replaced 'Israel' with 'Ireland', claiming that God would establish His throne here in this land forever. Clonmacnoise is located in County Offaly. However, Offaly is not the original name for the county. Under English rule it was called King's County. So I declared that instead of it being the seat for a human king, that a throne for the King of kings would be established in its stead.

Following this, I went into a time of prayer to repent for all the things that had happened in this place. I was repenting for the mistakes made and the decisions taken and also for the people who chose to use religion in their fight against the will of God. I read out the verses from Ezekiel that God had given me while I had waited quietly in His presence.

> "But if a wicked person turns away from all the sins they have committed and keeps all my decrees and does what is just and right, that person will surely live; they will not die. None of the offenses they have committed will be remembered against them. Because of the righteous things they have done, they will live. Do I take any pleasure in the death of the wicked? declares the Sovereign Lord. Rather, am I not pleased when they turn

from their ways and live?" [Ezekiel 18:21-23 NIV]

"Therefore, you Israelites, I will judge each of you according to your own ways, declares the Sovereign Lord. Repent! Turn away from all your offenses; then sin will not be your downfall. Rid yourselves of all the offenses you have committed, and get a new heart and a new spirit. Why will you die, people of Israel? For I take no pleasure in the death of anyone, declares the Sovereign Lord. Repent and live!" [Ezekiel 18:30-32 NIV]

Although I believe that God allowed Cromwell to come to Ireland, I am sure that God took no pleasure in the death of any of the Irish people. We had been foolish and punishment had come. God had always wanted us to turn in repentance from our wickedness so that such things would never happen. I prayed and asked God to forgive the wickedness of Ireland, and, in particular, those people who brought destruction on the land. As I walked around the rest of the site, I continued to pray and to make declarations as the Holy Spirit led me.

Photos: window and door at Clonmacnoise

The second location that I needed to visit was of course St Mary's Abbey in Dublin, the place where 'Silken' Thomas launched the first rebellion against the English. Although from first appearances, you might conclude that his rebellion didn't have a religious root, do remember that it was an event that began at an abbey and so, in actual fact, a rebellious root was planted into religion. The effect was that afterwards all subsequent Irish rebellions were given religious support or were instigated as a result of religious motives. In my research, I had looked up details of the abbey online and had found a notice saying that the site was closed until further notice. I searched again and got the contact details and sent the people in charge an email. Here is their response:

Dear Michael,

St Mary's Abbey is still closed to the public due to on-going works, however we are hoping to provide a pre-booked tour service through St Audoen's Church Visitor Centre later this year, starting around June and continuing until September. We hope to confirm this in the next few weeks.

Immediately Edith and I prayed and asked God to make a way. We entered into negotiations, and thankfully we were eventually allowed entry into the building. God had made a way for us to get in. All that remains of the original building is simply a set of basement rooms. At the time of the rebellion, it would have looked very different. Below is an artist's impression of the abbey that was in a picture we saw while at the site.

While I stood outside waiting to be let in, I went ahead and started to pray and to read scripture. God only gave me one verse for this place. It was from the Book of Isaiah:

"In that day the glory of Jacob will fade; the fat of his body will waste away." [Isaiah 17:4 NIV]

Photo: old drawing of Saint Mary's Abbey

What was God saying through this verse? I remembered that Jacob was the man who had wrestled with the Lord and so God seemed to be saying that the wrestling (rebellion) would come to an end. In fact it was also that the glory of wrestling would fade, that the glory of rebellion would fade. We need to see our rebellion for what it truly was and not as a story told by some puffed up pride-filled republican. I prayed about this and repented for the rebellion that had occurred. Edith was also given some verses in regards to this place. They were also from Isaiah:

> "Come, all you who are thirsty, come to the waters; and you who have no money, come, buy and eat! Come, buy wine and milk without money and without cost. Why spend money on what is not bread, and your labour on what does not satisfy? Listen, listen to me, and eat what is good, and you will delight in the richest of fare. Give ear and come to me; listen, that you may live. I will make an everlasting covenant with you, my

faithful love promised to David. See, I have made him a witness to the peoples, a ruler and commander of the peoples. Surely you will summon nations you know not, and nations you do not know will come running to you, because of the Lord your God, the Holy One of Israel, for he has endowed you with splendour." Seek the Lord while he may be found; call on him while he is near. Let the wicked forsake their ways and the unrighteous their thoughts. Let them turn to the Lord, and he will have mercy on them, and to our God, for he will freely pardon. "For my thoughts are not your thoughts, neither are your ways my ways," declares the Lord. "As the heavens are higher than the earth, so are my ways higher than your ways and my thoughts than your thoughts. As the rain and the snow come down from heaven, and do not return to it without watering the earth and making it bud and flourish, so that it yields seed for the sower and bread for the eater, so is my word that goes out from my mouth: It will not return to me empty, but will accomplish what I desire and achieve the purpose for which I sent it. You will go out in joy and be led forth in peace; the mountains and hills will burst into song before you, and all the trees of the field will clap their hands. Instead of the thornbush will grow the juniper, and instead of briers the myrtle will grow. This will be for the Lord's renown, for an everlasting sign, that will endure forever."
[Isaiah 55:1-13 NIV]

As I read this out, I started to realise that God was removing the issues of rebellion that had begun right in this spot and was instead, replacing it with the promise of Isaiah 55. Interestingly enough it did agree with the verse that God had given me in Isaiah 17, because the last time I had come across that chapter, was when the Lord was speaking to me about the 'Harvest of Ireland'. Here in Isaiah 55 using the picture of rain and snow and how the land produces its harvest, He promises that His word will not return empty but would accomplish everything that He desired. The result would be natural joy and peace.

Photo: ceiling in Saint Mary's Abbey

When I wrote about the harvest in *The Harvest is Here*[16], this was certainly part of it. I said that a harvest would happen quickly and that it would be just as Jesus said, that we would harvest what others had planted [John 4:38]. Perhaps the blockage preventing the harvest lay right here, here where our rebellions had begun. Indeed, only a week ago, I was heading out to help my church reach out to the homeless of Dublin City. Instead of just 'going along' with things, I waited and listened for direction from the Holy Spirit and He gave me a glimpse of the harvest. I saw that if we turn from our rebellion from God, if we turn from our religiousness and follow Him instead of our programmes and our pre-determined ministries, then God will give us the harvest we seek.

At this time that I was thinking through these things, I heard a teaching that struck into my heart. This verse became important to me:

> "Elijah took twelve stones, one for each of the tribes descended from Jacob, to whom the word of the Lord had come, saying,

"Your name shall be Israel." [1 Kings 18:31]

It was important because it linked with the collection of the twelve stones on my journey to the fading of Jacob [Isaiah 17:4]. In this chapter, the twelve stones were used to form the base of an altar on which fire fell from heaven. I prayed, "Let these twelve stones that I am collecting be removed from Ireland and let the fire from heaven fall upon Ireland. Let the fire of God fill each of our hearts. Let all false worship and idolatry be done away with by the power of God."

Chapter Ten
Opening our eyes to see Jesus

Since the day of your salvation when you first believed, have you had any experiences with the Living Lord Jesus? How many have you had? Just a few, or have you had several encounters? It is very easy to forget that Jesus is alive today when, every week, we meet at church and just talk about someone and what He did two thousand years ago. When you look back at believers in the New Testament, people met with the risen Lord. However, when those people went to share the good news with others who had followed Christ before his crucifixion, some of them refused to believe it at first. We can follow these events in the Gospel of Mark:

> "When Jesus rose early on the first day of the week, he appeared first to Mary Magdalene, out of whom he had driven seven demons. She went and told those who had been with him and who were mourning and weeping. When they heard that Jesus was alive and that she had seen him, they did not believe it. Afterward Jesus appeared in a different form to two of them while they were walking in the country. These returned and reported it to the rest; but they did not believe them either. Later Jesus appeared to the Eleven as they were eating; he rebuked them for their lack of faith and their stubborn refusal

to believe those who had seen him after he had risen." [Mark 16:9-14 NIV]

Now imagine someone standing up during a church meeting and sharing about having an experience with Jesus the night before, saying that Jesus had come to his home and spoken to Him about how he should change his life. How would the people in that church react? Would they refuse to believe that this man had been visited by Jesus? In many churches today, they probably would! As we read, not all of the eleven remaining disciples believed the eye-witnesses who reported their experiences with Jesus. They didn't believe until Jesus finally came in person and rebuked them. You see, it's easy to deny what someone is saying if we depend on our own thinking. We might think, "Jesus didn't do that because He hasn't done that with me" or, "If Jesus was saying that, then He would also have said it to me". So, instead of listening to the person's experience with Jesus and learning from it and going on to seek our own experience, we hold back in caution, or worse still, in cynical judgement until the other person stops talking.

That was the exact same mindset that led our ancestors to hold on to the religion that they had (Catholicism) instead of accepting a new way forward when it was given (Protestantism). The people wanted to hold on to a religion that had left them subject to foreigners. In the same way, after the resurrection, some of the disciples decided to hang on to what they had (the time they had spent with Jesus before the cross) instead of accepting the new way forward, which meant believing that Jesus was raised from the dead and that they could continue to experience Him. These disciples could not see past the crucifixion. Similarly, the Irish could not see past the label 'English'. They were unable to see that it was religion that handed them over to be conquered in the first place. Imagine three men in a bar, Paul, Steve and Mike. Paul tells Steve to punch Mike. Mike, in resentment, holds a grudge against Steve for the assault rather than against Paul who was the instigator. It's not just a mental block but also a spiritual blindness that prevented them from the seeing the truth. The same blindness kept the disciples from seeing the Truth. Yet, I believe that Jesus is able to penetrate through that. Just as He appeared to those disciples, it is my prayer that Jesus will pierce through your doubts and concerns so that you too can have wonderful experiences with Him. My hope is that you too will be able to testify about Jesus from this day on through having daily experiences with Him;

I'd like to share briefly with you an encounter that I had with Jesus a couple of years ago. It happened right in the middle of a prayer meeting. I was so deeply with the Lord that I was laid out on the ground on my back. Then I felt a huge weight pressing on my body and I saw a vision of Jesus putting his foot on me to hold me down. Whilst there, He showed me two things. First, He showed me a vision of hell and there in hell I saw the faces of people I knew and they were going to eternal torment. Then Jesus took me and showed me a vision of heaven. He showed me the same people again and asked me what was I going to do to help them? As He began to leave, I begged Him to stay, pleading with Him because to be in His presence like this was such a wonderful thing for me. At that, He reassured me that He is always with me.

We are hearing reports that other people around the world have had similar experiences. We even hear that Jesus has appeared to non-Christians, to people who knew nothing of Him beforehand. What we need to do is to change our whole mindset and be confident that Jesus is with us right now. It would do us good even to sit and be still and think this through and soak in the reality of it. Then we might begin to realise that when we seek Jesus we will find Him and will have ongoing encounters with Him. Let us take a big step of faith and walk away from the enslavement of religion. Let us open our eyes to see Jesus reaching out to take us by the hand.

It has always been difficult for us to understand the fact that spiritual powers exist and that there is a spiritual dimension. This is because in this physical life we generally do not see such things at work or don't believe what the Bible teaches us. This goes beyond the problem of forgetting that Jesus is alive and able to speak to us. Sometimes we look at what others are doing or saying, and respond judgementally and act in judgement, when in reality we are not fighting against flesh and blood but against powers and principalities of darkness. We see this happening throughout our history. Revolutionaries in Ireland rose to fight against physical foes when the real truth was that it was the powers of darkness who were the ones doing the damage.

> "For our struggle is not against flesh and blood, but against the rulers, against the authorities, against the powers of this dark world and against the spiritual forces of evil in the heavenly realms." [Ephesians 6:12 NIV]

If we have not recognised the spiritual dynamics at work behind the physical then how can we ever hope to win a battle or, indeed, even a war. Sadly, it seems much easier for humans to go rushing in with guns rather than getting on their knees before God to look for solutions. Lat year when I visited a D-Day museum in Portsmouth, I met a retired soldier who had been badly treated in the war. He stated that he still hated the enemy so much that he would even now gladly pick up a gun and shoot at them. The loss that people feel during wartime can lead them to have a deep sense of anger and even hatred against those who did the damage. This is bound to happen unless God helps them to forgive their former enemies.

We might well wonder, then, why do countries consider bombing people at all if all their action achieves is hatred stirred up in the hearts of the survivors. You might kill an enemy but, as soon as you do, a hundred will rise up in his place. You might wipe out a rebel force but a nation could rise to take their place. The Allies defeated Germany in WWII, but seventy years later which country is one of the most powerful in the EU? Germany has come back and holds an authoritative role in Europe. In the same way, while the English recognised that they had gone into Ireland on several occasions in order to punish the Irish people for rebelling against God, they failed to understand that every person that they wounded, and who survived, would become rebellious towards them in their hearts, and that later this would materialise as rebellious actions. Not only this, but they did not recognise that for every sin (i.e. theft, murder, massacre) they committed to the Irish People would bear spiritual consequences for them. In fact England failed to recognise God's long-term plan for Ireland and still fails to recognise it. The Irish had failed to open their eyes and see Jesus but so too had the English.

Just as physical rebellion is born out of hurt, hatred, loss and frustration, the same can be true of spiritual rebellion. Perhaps something bad happened to us as a child and so we think there is no God. Perhaps a loved one died from a disease and we wonder how God could allow this. Perhaps life isn't going our way and so we are frustrated and question why God made us the way we are. Whatever situation we find ourselves in, God has the answer. At one point in my own life, I asked God, "How much do you love me?" He responded by taking me back in a vision to all the worst times in my life and said to me these words, "Even then I had a plan for you." I could do nothing but cry as I realised that my problem was not God. Trust me, at times in my life, I was angry at God and certainly expressed my anger but now I could see that the problem was actually me. God had the solution but my refusal, as a result of my hurt and anger, was keeping me away from the solution. In the same way the people of Ireland burned with hurt and anger and, because of it, they have been unable to see God's solution.

> "What causes fights and quarrels among you? Don't they come from your desires that battle within you? You desire but do not have, so you kill. You covet but you cannot get what you want, so you quarrel and fight. You do not have because you do not ask God. When you ask, you do not receive, because you ask with wrong motives, that you may spend what you get on your pleasures." [James 4:1-3 NIV]

In Irish history, religion made the argument that rebellion was a 'just cause' and people easily believed this because of their anger and frustration. In the church today we see the same kind of thing when there is rebellion within the ranks because churches aren't operating according to Scripture. So let us be clear about this. One of the most common causes of disagreement in a church is the subject of worship. Pastors and worship-leaders often end up in heated debates about what songs should be played during a service or how many songs should be played and in what sequence. Picture for a moment you as an outsider called in to intervene in the situation. You could say that the pastor is the authority in the church and therefore he is right. Alternatively, you could say that the worship-leader specialises in this area and so what he is saying must be right. However, the physical truth is not the same as the spiritual truth. Both the pastor and the worship-leader have taken up what they believe to be a just cause when, in actual fact, their personal feelings or beliefs on the matter have no relevance. The only thing that matters is what pleases God and brings glory to His name. Their goal should be to fellowship together in prayer and seek God for the answer. This principle applies in other areas of church-life too. Debates and arguments are usually caused by someone seeking to control how things are done, or to prove the superiority of a particular theological point of view.

In such instances, people start to call in allegiant people to help them. The pastor could, for example, call on the elders of the church or other senior church figures to support his position. The worship-leader on the other hand may call on the rest of the worship-team, or supportive elders. He could even point to other churches in order to give examples of why the worship time should be different. But, in the end, the only allegiance that matters is allegiance to God, and no person has a monopoly on hearing what God is saying to the church. What other people think, what other leaders do, how other churches are run has no bearing on God's way forward for this particular church. God's ways are just God's ways! Either the two people in conflict are willing to seek God together about the matter or they are not. If they are not, then they are both in rebellion against God. If one is willing and the other is not, then the one who is not is the one in rebellion. If it's the pastor who's in rebellion then this will have serious consequences for the church. A church that is led by a person living in rebellion against God cannot be headed in the right direction. Jesus called such people 'blind guides':

> "Leave them; they are blind guides. If the blind lead the blind, both will fall into a pit." [Matthew 15:14 NIV]

Even the act of calling on supporters during an argument may well be a sign of rebellion against God. If we really believe that God is our Saviour, then let Him be our salvation in this instance too. Why do we need to call in supporters? If we are doing God's will, then surely God will send people to support us or to say the same things that we are saying. If we trust in human support to rescue us in difficulty, then where is our trust in God? How real is our salvation? Can we not pray like the psalmist? When he was afraid, he put his trust in God. This was how he conquered his fears and dealt with the enemies attacking him.

> "Be merciful to me, my God, for my enemies are in hot pursuit; all day long they press their attack. My adversaries pursue me all day long; in their pride many are attacking me. When I am afraid, I put my trust in you. In God, whose word I praise— in God I trust and am not afraid. What can mere mortals do to me?" [Psalm 56:1-4 NIV]

The only way a cause can be considered a just cause is if it is God's cause. If one wins an argument but the outcome is not of God then consequences will follow. There are always consequences to sinful actions. Our history tells us that. The history of other nations tells us that. Even our own personal history tells us that. Working alongside other believers is bound to result in conflicts along the way but we must handle these in the way God has shown us, always remembering that He is watching over us and is always willing to help us [Psalm 46:1].

Sometimes we do not even need other people in order to end up in rebellion. I once heard it said that, as soon as God gives you a promise, He will immediately remove any chance of you fulfilling that thing by yourself. This was certainly true for Abraham. It was only when he submitted to God that the promise of a son was given and Isaac was born. If it's God's promise then He will do it, not us. It is not by our methods or by our controls but by an ongoing submission to God that the promise can be fulfilled. No submission means no fulfilment! Total submission means total fulfilment! Why does God do it this way? He does it this way so He will get the glory and not us.

This is how things often work out:

a) God gives us a promise; we make plans, some out of submission and some out of our own understanding.
b) God makes it known that He is in charge by not allowing things to go as we planned.
c) We panic and go into 'emergency mode' because we feel our plans are going to fail.
d) At this point we have the opportunity to repent for taking a wrong direction and put our trust in God afresh.
e) God reveals His way forward.
f) His plan exceeds the original plan that we had created.
g) The promise is fulfilled.

From our prayer journey, Edith and I learnt a little about what God has in store for those who are seeking Him with a right heart. What I mean by 'a right heart' is that all wrestling with God has ceased and 100% submission has taken place. This is a tough thing for us all to do. We all have things in our lives that we love to do, possessions we hold dearly, and people we cherish. To lay everything aside, just as Christ did, means that we would be willing and even joyful should we lose it all. This is not a hypothetical situation either. Rest assured, God will test our hearts in every area to help us to be sure that we are willing to sacrifice everything in order to have Him. If we come through that testing by holding on in faith then His light will shine on our ways and our hearts will be refreshed, revived and renewed. Fire will even fall from heaven and set us aflame with God's love. The harvesters of the last revival in human history are to come by way of this process. Will we make it? Will we be one of them?

> *Then I heard a declaration that a song shall go forth like the sound of joyful birds in the morning sun and the song shall be of*

*love like the bride sings to her groom. Then, in a vision, I saw a great table for the wedding feast but the table was empty and I heard the Lord speak to the harvesters, "Go out into the field and gather the crops." I watched as the workers went out to work under the blue sky above their heads. I looked at them as they walked past me and they were of all sorts of people: young and old, experienced and beginners, educated and uneducated, men, women and children. Yet, in their eyes I saw a burning flame of determination and I heard a voice say, "These are the ones who will share my love, not religion." I noticed that not one of them took along a portion of bread or water. Instead they said, "My Lord will sustain me" [**Lamentations 3:24**]. However, they do take with them the new wine so that it will be brought to maturity whilst they work [**John 2:10**]. I watched as heaven became almost silent I saw the angels and the martyrs looking on for they had waited a long time for this day.*

*As the last harvester went forth, I saw a great assembly of angels gather and head out to assist the harvesters [**Psalm 91:11**] [**Hebrews 1:14**]. There was no set number of angels allocated to the individual harvesters. Some harvesters had but a few angels yet others were given many. The assigned number of angels provided the perfect balance for the harvesters to achieve their goals. Even though each harvester was to collect, he did not know how much he would collect but the Father in heaven knew all and He expected a complete delivery. For there is only one wedding feast such as this [**Revelation 19:9**], and the greatest harvest of all had been kept for such a time as this.*

I watched the harvesters hard at work. Others who saw them at work in the field came and asked "Can I also help to bring in the harvest?" So the number of harvesters grew although not all had been appointed from the start. The newcomers could harvest but not with the same anointing. As the harvest was being cut a new scent filled the air and it drifted up to heaven and was pleasing to the Lord as He waited. There were no limits set that held people back with assumptions of their ability. I saw children finding a large field and reaping a huge crop for the kingdom. It didn't matter not that they were young. In another place, I saw generation after generation going into fields together and working it side by side so that maximum yields could be taken. Blessed are those generations and blessed are the hands of those who work the fields for their names are written in heaven.

*Then the day came for the groom to leave His room [**Joel 2:16**]. He went out into the field and told those in charge, "Now is the time to bring all that is harvested and take it to the wedding feast" [**Joel 2:24**]. Then He went into the garden and said to the gardener "Bring the flowers to the feast, those without blemish that are in the fresh soil."*

*Lastly, I saw the groom set out to meet with His lover, His bride, and although she had waited for him, she did not know when He would arrive. She was glad to see Him come as she had been waiting in anticipation [**Revelation 19:7**]. He took her by the hand for she was without blemish and ready for intimacy and He said "Come, see the place that I have prepared for you" [**John 14:3**]. He took her into the feast room and they celebrated together in the midst of the greatest harvest and the perfect flowers. They ate rich food and drank of the new wine which had matured during the harvest [**Isaiah 25:6**]. [Extract from 'The Harvest is Here'[16]]*

Chapter Eleven
Religion sold us into slavery
Dublin & Galway

In chapter eight we saw the immediate effects of rebellion against God on our land and the consequences of that rebellion was explored in chapter nine. However, further to the immediate effects of rebellion, there were also other events that took place and which are of importance. These stem from the same roots of rebellion that we have already encountered yet, because these events are deemed so shocking, they have ended up dealt with as a separate part of this journey.

In recent years, historians have begun to uncover the fact that many people were taken as slaves from Ireland. The slavery we are referring to began early in the 17th century and continued being practiced until England outlawed it. I think that the key to understanding why this happened is found in Deuteronomy chapter 28 where the people were presented with a choice. They could either follow God and receive His blessing for their obedience or disobey Him and face His curse for rebellion against Him. An extract from the curse:

> "Your sons and daughters will be given to another nation, and you will wear out your eyes watching for them day after day,

powerless to lift a hand. A people that you do not know will eat what your land and labour produce, and you will have nothing but cruel oppression all your days. The sights you see will drive you mad. The Lord will afflict your knees and legs with painful boils that cannot be cured, spreading from the soles of your feet to the top of your head. The Lord will drive you and the king you set over you to a nation unknown to you or your ancestors. There you will worship other gods, gods of wood and stone. You will become a thing of horror, a byword and an object of ridicule among all the peoples where the Lord will drive you. You will sow much seed in the field but you will harvest little, because locusts will devour it. You will plant vineyards and cultivate them but you will not drink the wine or gather the grapes, because worms will eat them. You will have olive trees throughout your country but you will not use the oil, because the olives will drop off. You will have sons and daughters but you will not keep them, because they will go into captivity."
[Deuteronomy 28:32-41 NIV]

Following Cromwell's victory, many of the defeated soldiers were captured and interned in gaols and camps across Ireland. It is believed that there were between 34,000 and 40,000 prisoners held in detention. The war had been a huge expense to England and the ongoing upkeep of these camps was an expense that the exchequer did not want on his books so a solution to the problem was needed. The option eventually taken by the authorities was to give these prisoners the opportunity to leave Ireland and go abroad to fight in Spain and other countries, and indeed many decided to take this offer. Just to mention two of the migrations, 10,000 went off to fight in Spain and another 5,000 left to fight in Poland. It is quite possible that Cromwell would have preferred to have them all shipped to the West Indies to the plantations but there were simply too many of them and the last thing Barbados, or any other island, needed was for 50,000 Irish fighting men to come when they might revolt and seize the island. As these men left Ireland, they left behind their wives and children and their families which they probably never saw again. This was not the only problem facing Ireland at that time. In the ten years since the rebellion of 1641, one third of the population of 1.6 million had died due to the war, famine, disease and other hardships.

However, England was still not content despite winning the war and was already introducing laws that caused huge distress and destruction. In 1652, they passed 'The act of good affection' which essentially meant that most of the remaining population had to move to Connaught from wherever they lived. Everyone was included except those who had supported Cromwell in Dublin and Derry. It was also accepted that some of the common people could stay, to do jobs that the English did not want to do such as farming. For the people who arrived in Connaught, they were only given 10% of what they had previously owned. So, if they had owned 400 acres, they would now be given just 40 acres.

Due to the enormous resentment of this injustice, small bands of rebels started to carry out hit-and-run attacks on the English. They became known as the 'Tories'. When the English failed to track them down, they decided to arrest and punish people from local areas instead. Those captured were either hung or sent off to Barbados as slaves.

Selling people into slavery may have started as a punishment but England soon realised that there was money to be made of shipments of Irish slaves to Barbados and various other locations to work on the plantations. Soon afterwards, offers were made to the Irish to go abroad as 'indentured servants', which essentially meant that each person would enter into slavery for seven years and, at the end of the term, earn his or her freedom and acquire a small plot of land in the West Indies or North America. In reality however, while some chose freely, others were tricked and still others were kidnapped and deported as indentured servants. In spite of being told that they would have a good life in the plantations, when people arrived there (assuming they had survived the journey) they found themselves being worked to the bone, working up to seventeen hours a day and expected to survive on minimal provisions.

As well as this, some companies applied for a licence to take slaves from Ireland and this was granted by the English government. In search of slaves, they would come ashore and kidnap or trick those people who were most vulnerable such as women and children left abandoned by soldiers who had gone abroad, or those left as widows and orphans as a result of the war. The captured Irish fetched £4 a head at the port towns and cities such as Wexford and Waterford. At times, the governors of places such as Carlow or Kilkenny were instructed to arrest 'wanderers', whether men, women or children, and deliver them to the ports for deportation. It is possible that up to 100,000 children were shipped out of Ireland during this period of history.

These unfortunate 'wanderers' may have been living on the edge of Irish society and it was reported that some had even turned to cannibalism in order to survive. However, once captured or tricked into slavery, they faced an even worse fate. Barbados then was not anything like it is today. It was a tough place for those who ended up there and disease breakouts were common. The treatment of the Irish is claimed by some to have been considerably worse than that of the African slaves with their religion being a factor in how they were treated. All kinds of abuse and detestable things were protected there which are simply too hideous to discuss here. There was no defence for these people as the local governments were mainly run by the plantation owners who would naturally stand up for each other in court. Those indentured servants who got into trouble could have their terms of servitude extended. In fact, there was not much difference between these 'indentured servants' and the slaves except that the servants could eventually go free.

Of course, how the English treated the Irish at this time was contrary to the standard of religion given to us in the Bible:

> "External religious worship (religion as it is expressed in outward acts) that is pure and unblemished in the sight of God the Father is this: to visit and help and care for the orphans and

widows in their affliction and need, and to keep oneself unspotted and uncontaminated from the world." [James 1:27 AMP]

While large shipments of slaves departed from Ireland during this period of time, the story of slavery did not begin with Cromwell. We must remember that slavery had been evident in Ireland for a long time before this. Not only was Ireland raided by others for slaves but Ireland also used to raid other countries such as Wales and England in order to capture slaves. This is how Saint Patrick first came to Ireland. He came as a slave. In truth, we Irish are both victim and villain. When the New World, the West Indies and America, opened up new opportunities, new policies were brought in by the English and shipments of slaves from Ireland to America and the West Indies were already in place by 1620 under the rule of James I. Later, Charles I and Charles II continued this practice. This method of punishment was certainly well known in Ireland and was even mentioned in the document formulated at the Synod of Clonmacnoise. If you remember this synod that we discussed earlier, you may recall that the religious authorities were willing to proclaim Charles I as their king. This was the same person who would so easily send the Irish people into slavery. It may have been the accepted social punishment of the day, however, we must remember that each person sold as a slave was deeply loved by God.

God's love for people in slavery was shown through the lives of men like John Perrot, a Quaker who had a heart of compassion for them. He travelled to the West Indies and spent his life trying to help them, often at huge risk to his own life. At times, he was imprisoned, yet he still pressed on. He managed to make bargains and get child slaves set free and to get many adults who were slaves to be reclassified as indentured servants. How wonderful it is that, despite punishing Ireland for its rebellion against Him that God still wanted to send hope and relief to the Irish in their time of suffering.

By the middle of the 19th Century, abolition of slavery had begun and was spreading across the world. The shipment of slaves from Ireland to

America and the West Indies ceased but a new type of slavery, just as harsh, had already begun. It seems that the religious spirits instigating the sending of Irish people into slavery were not content to let slavery come to an end and in its place they used the hearts and minds of religious Irish people to enslave women and children right here within our own land.

By the middle of the 1700s a great distaste towards mothers of what were then termed 'illegitimate children' had developed in Irish society. Many of us have seen the film 'The Magdelene Sisters'[10], where we are told the story of some of the women who had been sent to live in asylums. Also, recently we heard about a mass grave of babies that was discovered in County Galway and which was subsequently investigated by the Gardai. It seems that both women and children were made to suffer just as they had been treated previously during the period of plantation slavery. The women were made to live asylums and many even spent the remainder of their lives working there under very harsh conditions. No repentance of their sins was allowed. Instead punishment upon punishment was inflicted on them. Many of these women were abused during their stay in these asylums, and you can see comparisons with the abuse of the Irish slaves in the plantations. Sexual abuse, verbal abuse, hard labour and poor living conditions became the story of so many unfortunate mothers and mothers-to-be.

Historians estimate that up to 30,000 women were confined in asylums in Ireland. The first asylum founded by Lady Arabella Denny opened on Leeson Street, Dublin in 1765, and the last one closed in 1996. That represents 231 years of neglect of Irish women and children. There is an interesting question, though, which we may ask. What happened to the men who had been in relationships with these women? It seems unreasonable to think that they went on to live out their lives without ever even passing a thought about the woman and her child. In the Bible, God teaches us that, when a man and woman come together, they become one. This one-ness is a spiritual tie which still exists whether a couple were legally married or not. Of course, without a marriage before God, there are consequences for the couple involved, but we won't go into that here. I just want to point out each of the men involved have been affected by that would have felt a spiritual tie for the rest of his life. It may have given them a sense of longing or wondering or even guilt.

The harsh treatment in the asylums created a fear amongst women in society. So great was this fear, that, if women got pregnant outside of marriage, they would hide the fact as well as they could. If they managed to do this until the child reached full term then, quite often there was no way for them to raise their child. Some of these babies were left at the doorsteps of houses and sadly, in other cases, the new mothers would kill their babies out of sheer desperation. Between 1922 and 1950, a hundred and eighty-three single mothers stood trial for the murder of their 'illegitimate' newborn babies at the Central Criminal Court in Dublin. What a staggering figure! Of course, this figure only represents those who got found out. Obviously there were many others children whose deaths went undetected.

However, it seems that Lady Arabella Denny actually acted with a good heart. She was well recognised for her charitable contributions and for her work to improve conditions in hospitals and workhouses. Such was the volume of her contributions that she was even visited by John Wesley in 1783. The original plan for the building on Leeson Street was to use it to help women in need, those who had 'fallen' or who were prostitutes. The charity offered the women accommodation, clothing, food and teaching about Jesus. The Magdalene asylums originated in England and this first Irish institution that was established was for Protestant girls. However, the Catholic Church soon followed suit and established similar organisations. Since the closing of these institutions, the Irish Government has admitted partial blame for the ill-treatment of women and children in these institutions and, in 2013, they issued a public apology and proceeded to set up a compensation scheme for the survivors. Yet there remains both a physical and a spiritual leftover from this abuse and even to this day, the location of the first Magdalene asylum in Dublin, Leeson Street, is linked with promiscuous women and remains the unofficial 'red light district' of the city.

In 1993, a mass grave containing the remains of 155 women was discovered at High Park Magdalene Laundry in Drumcondra. Their bodies were exhumed so that the Sisters of Our Lady of Charity could sell the land. These women had died during in their 'enslavement' at the laundry and their deaths had been kept secret. Even more recent was the discovery in Tuam, County Galway of a mass grave containing the remains of 796 children. Nearby was the location of a home for unmarried mothers dating from the 1920s to the 1960s. The bodies of these children were found piled up inside a septic tank. I don't believe that these discoveries and truths that are coming out in our day are co-incidences. I believe they are happening because innocent blood calls out from the earth for justice, just as it did in the days of Cain and Abel:

> "The Lord said, "What have you done? Listen! Your brother's blood cries out to me from the ground." [Genesis 4:10 NIV]

In recent years, many people have been engaged in interceding and repenting for Ireland. I believe this is why these secrets have come to light. God wants us to know the awful truth of how our forebears and our fellow-countrymen treated people who had made wrong choices in life so that we can repent of all the wrongs inflicted on them.

It is evident that there was a failure here on the part of individuals, the families and also the religious organisations as well as the state. Spiritually speaking, if an individual makes a mistake and then repents of his or her failure to obey God, then the matter should be settled. However, due to the strict religion of the period, so much more was demanded from people that parents even left their daughters at these institutions never to see them again. Imagine if, when we committed our first sin, God then took us and sent us to hell without any chance of repentance or hope of reprieve. These parents did not act in love but in blind obedience to religious spirits. In fact, the religious organisations were simply too religious. Love and mercy were rarely in evidence. It is easy for believers to look down at other people and pass judgement on them, which is what happened here. These women were not loved with the love of Jesus. Instead, they were enslaved by judgemental people who had never truly understood God's love. Once again, what James wrote is relevant here:

> "External religious worship (religion as it is expressed in outward acts] that is pure and unblemished in the sight of God the Father is this: to visit and help and care for the orphans and widows in their affliction and need, and to keep oneself unspotted and uncontaminated from the world." [James 1:27 AMP]

The religious and cultural system, which was a worldly system, was determined to judge and punish women who they saw as sinful. However, we are told to keep ourselves uncontaminated from the world. A parent with an uncontaminated heart filled with the love of Jesus would never assign their daughter to life in an asylum. A person with an uncontaminated heart would never have enslaved and abused vulnerable women like these.

I spent some time talking to God about all of these things, in particular asking God to show us the locations in Ireland that we should travel to in order to repent for the rebellion that led to our enslavement. I struggled with this for a variety reasons. Firstly, there is no definitive place in the country where slavery began and so originating places were difficult to identify. Then, one day, I woke up after having a dream where I was told simply this, "Go to Dublin and then to Galway". In my thinking, I began to consider locations such as Tuam or Leeson Street where we could go and pray. But I stopped thinking like this when God led me to this verse in the Psalms:

> "As far as the east is from the west, so far has he removed our transgressions from us." [Psalm 103:12 NIV]

What God was wanting us to do was to travel from Dublin to Galway, from coast to coast, to declare countrywide that God is removing our transgression and forgiving our rebellion and enslavement. He also showed me this verse:

> "So if the Son sets you free, you will be free indeed." [John 8:36

NIV]

Photo: Killiney beach

In response to God's direction, Edith and I started out by heading to Killiney beach in Dublin. It had been several years since I had been there but I found it okay and parked for free because it was on a Sunday. As we walked out onto the beach we saw a lovely view. Edith and I stood there together and began to pray and make prophetic declarations based upon the above verse in the Psalms while repenting for all the horrible sins inflicted on women and children all across this land. Our attention was drawn to the waves breaking along the shore and Edith had a verse come to her heart from Corinthians, so we began to declare it for Ireland and for the Irish people:

> If Irish people come into Christ, they are a new creation: The old has passed away, the new has come. [Based on 2 Corinthians 5:17]

Edith began to prophesy that the waves were refreshing, that each wave was individual and unique and they were washing the land.

From there were travelled on to Galway just as I had been shown to do in my dream. We continued to hold onto the phrase 'from the east to the west' in our hearts as we travelled. While driving, I felt that we should play an old recording that had been made in 2013 when Chuck Pierce visited Ireland. We found it in the car and played it and listened to the words afresh. In one particular spot, Chuck declared that, "The captivity that Ireland has been in will come to an end." This statement struck a chord with me as we have been praying and fasting and following God's leading so that the oppression or 'captivity' of Irish people by religion might be broken off from us.

When we arrived in Galway we headed straight for Salthill which as I knew would be the nearest beach. We noticed some similarities between the two areas. They were both areas where tourists came and were also both areas of wealth. Perhaps there was some meaning to this wealth that I did not understand on the day. Perhaps it reflected the wealth that was gathered from the selling of people as slaves.

Photo: Salthill beach

We parked the car and prayed together and thanked God for the day and for removing the stain of these transgressions from our land. Then, we ate some fruit and prayed as we declared that Ireland would now bear much fruit that God had removed these transgressions.

Chapter Twelve
Your Children will ask

In the U.S. the Southern Baptist Council found that 88% of children raised in evangelical homes left their churches at the age of 18, never to return$_6$. What is it that causes us Christians to lose our children to the enemy? I think that the key is that we are failing to do is highlighted by the verse below. God told Moses that they were to celebrate the Passover when they reached the Promised Land and make sure to explain the meaning of it to their children:

> "And when your children ask you, 'What does this ceremony mean to you?'" [Exodus 12:26 NIV]

Why would the children have needed to ask such a question? We might imagine that they would grow up observing the yearly rituals carried out by their people, and that they would be present while each part of the Passover meal was enacted. Yet still, we can expect that they would have had this question in their minds, "What does it all mean?"

In 2013, I had the opportunity to travel to Herrnhut in Germany. The story of what happened there in the 18th century, the revival and the beginning of the modern mission movement is well documented. But there was also a prayer meeting that began at that time and continued for over a hundred years maybe even as long as a hundred and twenty years. While I was there, I asked, "Why did the prayer stop?" I was told that, as succeeding generations came along, they couldn't understand why they were praying. They knew that people before them had prayed and so they carried on and filled the time-slots that were allocated. However, over time, the prayer that was begun as a desperate call to God during a time of persecution became just a monotonous prayer-time with religiously allocated time-slots. Eventually these people asked, "What does this mean?" By then, the prayer meant nothing to them. It had become an empty ceremony that they probably found old and outdated. So, they stopped praying.

Something seems to get lost between one generation and another but how does that happen? What can we do to change things so that we do not have to watch our children being taken over by another kingdom as soon as they turn eighteen? I sought God and asked him, "What is it in our method of teaching that we must change? What is it that we are doing wrong that is driving our children to death and a cursed existence?" You see, the danger is that children can attend our church meetings with us. They may hear the word of God and sing along with the songs but their experience of church is mere religion. After seeking God, I knew that we needed to examine how God teaches us and then apply His methods to how we teach our children.

So, let's see how God teaches us from the example of Him providing for Moses and His people in the desert:

> "Then Moses led Israel from the Red Sea and they went into the Desert of Shur. For three days they travelled in the desert without finding water. When they came to Marah, they could not drink its water because it was bitter. (That is why the place is called Marah.) So the people grumbled against Moses, saying, "What are we to drink?" Then Moses cried out to the Lord, and the Lord showed him a piece of wood. He threw it into the water, and the water became fit to drink. There the Lord issued a ruling and instruction for them and put them to the test. He said, "If you listen carefully to the Lord your God

> and do what is right in his eyes, if you pay attention to his commands and keep all his decrees, I will not bring on you any of the diseases I brought on the Egyptians, for I am the Lord, who heals you." Then they came to Elim, where there were twelve springs and seventy palm trees, and they camped there near the water." [Exodus 15:22-27 NIV]

The Israelites had just come out of Egypt and they did not know much about God and so they were completely dependent on Moses for guidance. Their nation was like a new-born baby brought home by his father to the family with the older brother being given responsibility to help them on their journey of learning. In these verses we see that the Israelites had a very important problem to be solved - to find a source of drinking water. We humans, cannot survive without water for more than a few days and so I am sure that they were very pleased when they found water at Marah and yet all the more irate when they realised that the water was bitter and they would not be able to drink it. But Moses called out to God and God provided the solution they needed. My question is, "Why didn't they just find fresh water ready to drink?" God could have easily gone ahead of them and made the water fresh. It was because God wanted His people to learn that, if they called out to Him in need, then He would hear them and answer their prayer.

In the Gospel of John, we read that Jesus' first miracle was when He turned water into wine at a wedding feast:

> "When the wine was gone, Jesus' mother said to him, "They have no more wine." "Woman, why do you involve me?" Jesus replied. "My hour has not yet come." His mother said to the servants, "Do whatever he tells you." Nearby stood six stone water jars, the kind used by the Jews for ceremonial washing, each holding from twenty to thirty gallons. Jesus said to the servants, "Fill the jars with water"; so they filled them to the brim. Then he told them, "Now draw some out and take it to the master of the banquet." They did so, and the master of the banquet tasted the water that had been turned into wine. He

did not realise where it had come from, though the servants who had drawn the water knew. Then he called the bridegroom aside and said, "Everyone brings out the choice wine first and then the cheaper wine after the guests have had too much to drink; but you have saved the best till now." [John 2:3-10 NIV]

We can see immediately that there is a similarity between these two situations. Here again, there was a practical need; the wine had run out. Mary came to Jesus and explained the problem. He first replied by saying that His time had not yet come, but then responded to the need and turned the water into wine that proved to be the best wine tasted at the feast. This example is connected to the spiritual significance of Jesus coming for his own wedding feast. However, let's look at some more examples of this 'needs-based' teaching. Let's examine another incident in the desert where, this time, God provided food for His people. Once again, we find the Israelites complaining:

> "In the desert the whole community grumbled against Moses and Aaron. The Israelites said to them, "If only we had died by the Lord's hand in Egypt! There we sat around pots of meat and ate all the food we wanted, but you have brought us out into this desert to starve this entire assembly to death." Then the Lord said to Moses, "I will rain down bread from heaven for you. The people are to go out each day and gather enough for that day. In this way I will test them and see whether they will follow my instructions. On the sixth day they are to prepare what they bring in, and that is to be twice as much as they gather on the other days." So Moses and Aaron said to all the Israelites, "In the evening you will know that it was the Lord who brought you out of Egypt, and in the morning you will see the glory of the Lord, because he has heard your grumbling against him. Who are we, that you should grumble against us?" [Exodus 16:2-7 NIV]

> "That evening quail came and covered the camp, and in the morning there was a layer of dew around the camp. When the

> dew was gone, thin flakes like frost on the ground appeared on the desert floor. When the Israelites saw it, they said to each other, "What is it?" For they did not know what it was. Moses said to them, "It is the bread the Lord has given you to eat. This is what the Lord has commanded: 'Everyone is to gather as much as they need. Take an omer for each person you have in your tent.' " The Israelites did as they were told; some gathered much, some little." [Exodus 16:13-17 NIV]

On this occasion, the Israelites were hungry and, once again, they complained against Moses. In response, Moses delivered a message to them from God saying that they were going to have plenty of food. They would only receive enough for one day at a time except on the day before the Sabbath when they would get enough for two days. Here we can see that the lesson God is teaching has moved on from, "Call to Me and I will answer you" to "You need to seek Me each day for what you need".

Let's look at a similar example from the way that Jesus taught His disciples at the feeding of the five thousand:

> "When Jesus looked up and saw a great crowd coming toward him, he said to Philip, "Where shall we buy bread for these people to eat?" He asked this only to test him, for he already had in mind what he was going to do. Philip answered him, "It would take more than half a year's wages to buy enough bread for each one to have a bite!" Another of his disciples, Andrew, Simon Peter's brother, spoke up, "Here is a boy with five small barley loaves and two small fish, but how far will they go among so many?" Jesus said, "Have the people sit down." There was plenty of grass in that place, and they sat down (about five thousand men were there). Jesus then took the loaves, gave thanks, and distributed to those who were seated as much as they wanted. He did the same with the fish. When they had all had enough to eat, he said to his disciples, "Gather the pieces that are left over. Let nothing be wasted." So they gathered

them and filled twelve baskets with the pieces of the five barley loaves left over by those who had eaten." [John 6:5-13 NIV]

Here we see Jesus teaching the disciples that God can provide all our needs if we trust in Him. From this and the other examples we have seen clearly that God uses 'needs based' teaching both in the Old Testament and the New Testament. God does not change, so we must assume that God still teaches today the exact same way. It is important to ask, why does God teach us this way rather than just giving us knowledge?

While studying for my degree, I spent a year specifically learning about child development. I found that it is through a needs-based process that babies learn to understand the relationship between them and their parents. As babies, we merely cry out because we feel hungry or thirsty but we don't know where our food will come from. All we know is that we have a need and that we don't know what to do about it. Then, as we receive that food for the first time and indeed the many times after that, we learn to be dependent on our earthly parents. This relationship of course changes as the child gets more understanding but the most basic and the most important lesson is that we have a need and that need is met. This has shown me that learning to be part of a spiritual family works in the same way. We must become like children. The most basic relationship that we need to start out with, therefore, is not a knowledge-based relationship but a needs-based one. Remember what Jesus said when he used the example of a young child:

> "Whoever will humble himself therefore and become like this little child (trusting, lowly, loving, forgiving) is greatest in the kingdom of heaven." [Matthew 18:4 AMP]

Jesus placed an emphasis here on the lesson we can learn from a child. He showed us that to be great in the kingdom of God meant that we should change and become trusting, lowly, loving and forgiving just like a child. To do this we need to learn to be dependent on God, our Father in heaven, and not solely upon our church or pastor. When we have a need, we need to get down on our knees and cry out to God and depend on Him for our provision. Learning to know God personally and intimately must be our priority. It is vital to have a close friendship with God and to maintain that relationship on a daily basis. Indeed, with our children, we need to introduce them to having this kind of relationship with God. I truly believe that knowing all of the stories in the Bible will never save a child from becoming one of those 88% who fall away. Instead, experiencing God through a needs-based relationship will help that child to grow in his or her faith. Knowledge and experience are two very different things. Consider this illustration:

Imagine that I was speaking at your church and that I had brought a famous footballer along with me. I get him to stand at the front to my left. Then on my right, I place a full-sized cardboard replica of him. Now tell me why should I introduce you to the cardboard image first, when the real person is standing right there within reach? If we as parents and as members of a church only manage to teach our children stories about God and if our children fail to experience God personally on their journey through life, then they won't get to know God at all. Here is a beautiful verse from 1 John that explains this. The word 'know' is expanded to help our understanding in the Amplified Version:

> "We are (children) of God. Whoever is learning to know God (progressively to perceive, recognise, and understand God by observation and experience, and to get an ever-clearer knowledge of Him) listens to us; and he who is not of God does not listen or pay attention to us. By this we know (recognise) the Spirit of Truth and the spirit of error." [1 John 4:6 AMP]

So here we see 'observation and experience' as being very important in order for us to learn how to know God. This makes sense considering that with other relationships, whether it be friends or family, is built upon our experiences with them. Whether you are a pastor, mentor, Sunday-school teacher or a parent, we must consider how we can facilitate and help the next generation to experience God. Consider the people of Israel at the time of the Exodus. They depended on Moses to pray and intercede for them whereas God wanted them individually to seek His face in the same way. God wants our children to seek Him individually. God wants the same for each and every child. He doesn't want our children to pray just because we have asked them or to attend events just because we bring them along in a car. God wants every child to turn to Him and develop their own personal relationship with Him.

God loves our children much more than we can ever love them and He has placed them into our care so that we can bring them up to be men and women who know God. Consider a prodigal son who has gone out into the wilderness of the world. The mother would obviously pray and yearn to see her son come home, but more importantly to turn back to God. How much more then, does God look forward to seeing a prodigal return home? If we, as parents introduce children to God rather than religion then they have a good chance of never becoming a prodigal. Therefore, I want my children to come to know God just like it says in 1 John 4:6 and be able to perceive, recognise and understand God through both observation and personal experience.

If you look at that verse in First John again, you may notice that there is a contrast here between the following two kinds of people and two spirits.

- People who are learning to know God are under the influence of the Spirit of Truth. They listen to what God has to say through people like John and others on the same journey.
- People who are not of God and do not listen to what God has to say. They are under the influence of the spirit of error.

This spirit of error is very easy to identify if we consider what people did in opposition to the teachings of Jesus. Several times He spoke out against people who were outwardly religious – who knew the law but did not know God. We can see examples of this in Matthew 6 & 7 in Jesus' Sermon on the Mount:

Firstly, let us look at what Jesus said about doing **charitable deeds:**

> "Be careful not to practice your righteousness in front of others to be seen by them. If you do, you will have no reward from

> your Father in heaven. So when you give to the needy, do not announce it with trumpets, as the hypocrites do in the synagogues and on the streets, to be honoured by others. Truly I tell you, they have received their reward in full. But when you give to the needy, do not let your left hand know what your right hand is doing, so that your giving may be in secret. Then your Father, who sees what is done in secret, will reward you." [Matthew 6:1-4 NIV]

Jesus clearly tells us here not to do good deeds in a boastful manner. What good is it if we pray with someone and they are healed, if we boast about what we have done afterwards? What good is it if we give large sums of money to the poor, if we boast about that too? Let us boast about nothing except what Jesus did! Let us ask ourselves, did we really do the work? Was it by our power that someone was healed? No, it was by the power of Jesus that the person was healed. Did you really give your own money, or did you allow God to provide for someone through you in the same way that He had provided for you through others?

Next, Jesus spoke about **prayer:**

> "And when you pray, do not be like the hypocrites, for they love to pray standing in the synagogues and on the street corners to be seen by others. Truly I tell you, they have received their reward in full. But when you pray, go into your room, close the door and pray to your Father, who is unseen. Then your Father, who sees what is done in secret, will reward you. And when you pray, do not keep on babbling like pagans, for they think they will be heard because of their many words. Do not be like them, for your Father knows what you need before you ask him." [Matthew 6:5-8 NIV]

Here Jesus instructs us not to pray in a way that shows off to others. We are told not to use empty words that may sound good to others but mean nothing by way of communicating with God. Consider this, when we come to pray, do we call out so that others around us will hear or do we call out so that Jesus will hear? Do we pray the same in front of others as we would when we pray when we are in a private room?

Following this, Jesus spoke about **fasting:**

> "When you fast, do not look sombre as the hypocrites do, for they disfigure their faces to show others they are fasting. Truly I tell you, they have received their reward in full. But when you fast, put oil on your head and wash your face, so that it will not be obvious to others that you are fasting, but only to your Father, who is unseen; and your Father, who sees what is done in secret, will reward you." [Matthew 6:16-18 NIV]

Here, Jesus warns us not to boast about our fasting. Are we fasting so that others will comment about how great we are for doing it? Or are we fasting to remind our bodies that we are spiritual beings and that we depend not on physical food but on the Word of God.

Then Jesus went on to speak about **wealth:**

> "Do not store up for yourselves treasures on earth, where moths and rust destroy, and where thieves break in and steal. But store up for yourselves treasures in heaven, where moths and vermin do not destroy, and where thieves do not break in and steal. For where your treasure is, there your heart will be also. "The eye is the lamp of the body. If your eyes are healthy, your whole body will be full of light. But if your eyes are unhealthy, your whole body will be full of darkness. If then the light within you is darkness, how great is that darkness! "No one can serve two masters. Either you will hate the one and love the other, or you will be devoted to the one and despise the other. You cannot serve both God and money." [Matthew 6:19-34 NIV]

If we find that we are turning from God to trust in other resources to meet our needs then our lives will cease to be focused on Him. We need to come to an understanding that everything we have was provided to us by our Father in heaven who loves us. We also need to be thankful for what we have and not be yearning for the things of this world. He tells us not to store up treasure on earth. We cannot take our wealth with us when we die. Can we bring any of our belongings with us such as our cars, our houses, our computers, CDs, or DVDs? If we are focused on possessing these earthly things, then our minds and hearts are not yearning to live a humble and obedient life that produces rich rewards in heaven.

Then Jesus spoke about **judging others:**

> "Do not judge, or you too will be judged. For in the same way you judge others, you will be judged, and with the measure you use, it will be measured to you. "Why do you look at the speck of sawdust in your brother's eye and pay no attention to the plank in your own eye? How can you say to your brother, 'Let me take the speck out of your eye,' when all the time there is a plank in your own eye? You hypocrite, first take the plank out of your own eye, and then you will see clearly to remove the speck from your brother's eye." [Matthew 7:1-5 NIV]

Jesus warns us not to judge others or else we will be judged. My brothers and sisters in Christ, do we talk about other Christians who have made a wrong step in a judgemental way or do we gather around them to love them and help them? Do we watch Youtube videos that criticise famous preachers when our focus is not to be on what others may be doing wrong, but on God, listening to Him and learning what we are to be doing with our own lives. God does not want us to get distracted by having a judgemental attitude and gossiping about others.

We must consider each of these five subjects carefully: charitable deeds, prayer, fasting, wealth and judging others. How we behave is important. We must remember that our children only see our actions and behaviours. They cannot see our mindset, our understanding or our feelings. Just because we understand and do things with a right heart does not mean that our children will understand why. They witness the visible, but still need to ask, "What does this ceremony mean?"

If all they see is a facade, and a form of religion that is empty, it will carry no impact on them! As well as that, they will tend to find the whole experience boring! I know many friends and family who grew up attending churches and then walked away from God. However, in reality, they were not walking away from God; they were turning away from empty religion. I can say that because I know that God is wonderful. He is amazing and never boring! If our children are bored, they are merely being exposed to empty religion and not God. We need to work hard at introducing them to God.

If our children only experience a religion and later walk away from it, they are like someone who has been inoculated. When you get an injection, a small trace of the disease in the solution enters your body, in order for your immune system to learn to fight it. If we give our children a dose of man-made religion, then they will learn to stand up to anyone who mentions God to them! Later in life, having grown to detest this kind of religiousness, and wrongly associating God with religious-hearted people they will brush away the attempts made by God to save them.

My conclusion is this: I don't want religion, I want God.

I don't want my children to be merely religious. I want them to know and love God!

When the time comes for our children to live independently, they can choose to continue on into the Promised Land and discover what God has in store for their lives. Whether they have been taught in truth or in error will impact on the choices they make. In a similar way, the Israelites came to the moment when they needed to step out in faith and trust in God. Instead they shrunk back because they did not really know God. If they did, they would have understood that His mighty power would make conquest possible for them and they would not have hesitated from entering the Promised Land. Only Joshua and Caleb had come to know and understand that if God was with them, then there was no need to fear.

"And they said (the people) to each other, "We should choose a leader and go back to Egypt." Then Moses and Aaron fell facedown in front of the whole Israelite assembly gathered there. Joshua son of Nun and Caleb son of Jephunneh, who were among those who had explored the land, tore their clothes and said to the entire Israelite assembly, "The land we passed through and explored is exceedingly good. If the Lord is pleased with us, he will lead us into that land, a land flowing with milk and honey, and will give it to us. Only do not rebel against the Lord. And do not be afraid of the people of the land, because we will devour them. Their protection is gone, but the Lord is with us. Do not be afraid of them." [Numbers 14:4-9 NIV]

The Lord replied:

"Not one of them will ever see the land I promised on oath to their ancestors. No one who has treated me with contempt will ever see it. But because my servant Caleb has a different spirit and follows me wholeheartedly, I will bring him into the land he went to, and his descendants will inherit it." [Numbers 14:23-24]

When we look back at the history of slavery in Ireland and mistreatment of children and women in this country we are bound to be shocked. But, in fact, it highlights the spiritual state of our modern church. Consider for a moment what slavery is. We could describe it as the throwing of one person into a cruel way of life by another. Whilst in that way of life, they get treated less well than others, not receiving full recognition for their work. Is this how children are being treated in our churches? When was the last time you saw a child lead worship? Or preach? Or evangelise? We are saying by our actions, "They are not able to do it". They are probably not able because we speak inability over them. They are not able because we do not enable them. They are not able because they are getting no experience. Surely, we don't want our children to go through church and walk into death on the other side.

If we are taking our children on spiritual journeys where they may die (just like the journeys of those who went to the West Indies on slave ships), then we are no better that the captains of those slave ships. Are we trying to teach our children through a form of coercion, trickery or forced involvement? Then we are no better than those who sold the children of Ireland into slavery. Do we give our children very little spiritual provisions? Are we telling them about God but not introducing them to Him? Then we are no better than the plantation owners who gave the slaves very little food. Do we ostracise our children if they turn away from church? Then we are no better than those people who ostracised unmarried mothers to the extent that they felt that they had to kill their children. Do we submit to the system of Sunday school, doing it because it is what has always been done, forcing children to attend, instead of seeking God about how to effectively teach children? Then we are no better than those authorities who gathered up vagrants and deported them.

We must admit our faults and flaws and allow God to save us from error. We must allow God to change us and our churches so that our children experience God personally for themselves. Let us not be obedient to empty religion, captured by our own enslavement, but rather, let us break free from all of that and bring our children with us.

Chapter Thirteen
Religion led us into pride
Áras an Uachtaráin, Dublin
Cavehill, Belfast

Once again we move forward in our journey and we will look at another part of our history and another spiritual root. Much of what we have covered so far in Irish history has concerned the religiousness of people who called themselves Roman Catholic but they weren't the only denomination that brought trouble to our shores. We must recognise the fact that people with religious hearts can be found in any denomination. Our modern churches, for example, are rife with such people. In this chapter we will see how Protestant pride became established and what trouble this brought to Ireland. Again we see a reference to this kind of situation in Deuteronomy Chapter 28:

> "The foreigners who reside among you will rise above you higher and higher, but you will sink lower and lower. They will lend to you, but you will not lend to them. They will be the head, but you will be the tail." [Deuteronomy 28:43-44 NIV]

In this part of our history that we are referring to, it was the Anglo-Irish Protestants who rose higher whilst the other denominations sank lower. They ran the country and at the same time held back every other denomination, in particular the Catholics, the Jews and the Presbyterians. Central to this repression were the Penal Laws which were passed in 1691. These laws were very much linked to what was happening politically in England after the Protestant King, William, deposed James II in 1688. The Jacobite claim to the throne had always been supported by the Pope and all Catholics were therefore obliged to do likewise. This was the political situation that had led to the previous war between England and Cromwell. The culmination of these events led to another war, the Williamite War, which was essentially a war of James versus William. However, the Jacobites were defeated here in Ireland, and England needed to make sure that no further rebellion or war would take place. The outcome was the introduction of the Penal laws which aimed at keeping Catholic political power under control.

During this period, the so-called Protestant Ascendancy developed and there were several great accomplishments in different areas of society. For example, *The Messiah*, written by Handel at the request of Charles Jennens, was performed for the first time in Dublin on 13th April 1742. There were also other achievements in areas such as poetry, literature, philosophy and architecture. There was stability and freedom from war and the Irish Volunteer Force, numbering about 100,000, was formed to protect Ireland from invasion during the American Civil War. From the 1780's, there was a massive economic boom which saw the establishment of the Four Courts and the General Post office in Dublin as well as extensions to the canals being built. Ireland was becoming a 'civilized country' and it was hoped that other nations such as England would no longer see the Irish people as savages. Despite these developments, much of the wealth generated in the country ended up in the hands of absentee landlords who lived in England and beyond. Sadly, there is only a thin line dividing thankfulness and pride. Jeremiah saw the dangers of pride, this is what he wrote:

> "This is what the Lord says: "Let not the wise boast of their wisdom or the strong boast of their strength or the rich boast of their riches, but let the one who boasts boast about this: that they have the understanding to know me, that I am the Lord,

who exercises kindness, justice and righteousness on earth, for in these I delight," declares the Lord." [Jeremiah 9:23-24 NIV]

The Book of Proverbs also warns us about the danger of pride:

"Pride goes before destruction, a haughty spirit before a fall." [Proverbs 16:18 NIV]

During 1783, Henry Grattan's government reached an agreement with England that allowed more powers for Ireland and Ireland became self-governing. Grattan did not want full separation from England because he saw the economic and geographic benefits of staying linked to them. However, he did want Ireland to rule itself and come out from under the control of the monarchy. His government also made progress towards relieving Irish people from the demands of the Penal laws. In reality, this was a minefield. It was difficult to make such choices to decide when and by how much should these laws be repealed. In effect, the relief only came in stages between 1778 and 1829.

Thrown into this mix was a man called Theobald Wolfe Tone who had been born in 1763 to a Protestant Dublin family. In 1791, he and some others formed the Society of United Irishmen. Their original aim was to bridge the gap between Irish Catholics and Protestants and to bring them into unity. In 1794 the society members were visited by the Reverend William Jackson, an Anglican preacher with particular political opinions. He came to Ireland to assess if Ireland might be willing to assist a French invasion of the country. The reason why Jesus gave the following instruction was also relevant in this context:

"Be careful," Jesus warned them. "Watch out for the yeast of the Pharisees and that of Herod." [Mark 8:15 NIV]

There are people who hold certain political and religious beliefs and Jesus warns us about such people. These are the same kind of people that crucified Jesus. It sounds great to want to bring unity between different believers. Yet, hidden behind their vocal aims were certain political ideas. We should, as Christians keep our seeking of God separate to any worldly aspirations. We must also keep watch that we are not caught up in the aspirations of others, which outwardly seem good, but secretly hide deception. To do this we must ensure that we are not affected by their yeast, as yeast spreads easily through all of the dough.

Following Jackson's visit, the Society became more and more frustrated by the lack of action of the Irish Parliament and began to consider what Jackson had said about a French invasion despite Jackson's capture and trial. In the aftermath of the trial, the Society's links to Jackson meant that Wolfe Tone and other leaders were to be exiled to America. However, before leaving, Wolfe Tone travelled to Cavehill in Belfast where he and other men dedicated themselves to a new cause – Irish Independence. When Wolfe Tone reached America he was still filled with the ideas of revolution and so he went from there to France to request an invasion force. Once there, he lied to the King, telling him in pride that Ireland was united and ready to fight against the English. As a result, 15,000 troops were granted and dispatched from Paris to Ireland. What the Bible says in the Book of Proverbs is particularly relevant here:

> "A troublemaker and a villain, who goes about with a corrupt mouth, who winks maliciously with his eye, signals with his feet and motions with his fingers, who plots evil with deceit in his heart— he always stirs up conflict. Therefore disaster will overtake him in an instant; he will suddenly be destroyed— without remedy." [Proverbs 6:12-15 NIV]

It's not that I would choose personally to call the founder of Irish republicanism a troublemaker and a villain. However, we must remember what rebellion is. It is denying that God has power over men to put them into power or to remove them. It means depending on human strength rather than God's and, according to Romans 13, it is actually rebellion against God. We know this to be true, that God is the ruler of both heaven and earth. In the Bible, Jesus could calm a storm by just speaking one word but, in this instance He sent a storm to thwart the progress of this invasion force. The storm lasted for several days and the French force had to return to where it had come from.

Then, in 1798, and without the support of the French fleet, the Society began a rebellion in Ireland. Wolfe Tone arrived later with a French force of 3,000 soldiers but was captured by the English and subsequently court-marshalled and hung for treason. Henry Joy McCracken, who had been present on the day when the men stood on Cavehill to make their declaration, was captured there on the hill after the failed rebellion. He was also court-marshalled and hung. His story is interesting because of what we have discovered in other areas of this journey. We found that the location something begins is quite often where it ends.

The 1798 rebellion was more than likely a bad course of action for Ireland as it is quite possible that Grattan's government would have eventually secured independence. Immediately after the rebellion, Home Rule was abandoned and the Act of Union was passed, placing Ireland, Scotland, Wales and England under direct rule from Westminster. Now, thanks to our pride, we would have new links with the 'enemy' that would be even more difficult to break and it would take more than a hundred years to do so.

I think these events this resonate with events in recent Irish history and the so called 'Celtic Tiger' that everyone so proudly boasted of during the so-called 'boom' years. If you look up the definition of religion you can see that things such as consumerism and globalisation can be described as a religion (religion is defined as an interest that is followed with great devotion). During the Protestant Ascendancy, one of the stated aims was to reach new levels of cultural and economic achievement. This is exactly what was said during the boom years here in Ireland. Ireland's economy grew at a rate of almost 10% per year, from 1995 to 2000, and then about 6% until the crash in 2008. Central to all of this was the decision by Ireland in 1973 to join the European Union (EU). The EU invested money in Ireland, helping us to improve our infrastructure and roads network. Simultaneously, Ireland opened up to foreign investment. A country, which previously had been mostly agricultural, now became more and more industrialised.

Since the crash, it has been easy for everyone to point the finger at the people we would like to hold responsible: the politicians, the bankers, the EU and several others. The truth, however, is that we all contributed to the economic boom and we boasted about how we had made money from it. For my part, I had bought a house around 1999 and sold it three years later making a profit of about €50,000 from the sale. That extra €50,000 needed to buy the exact same house I had bought is probably now owed by someone else to the failed banks. I believe we are all to blame for letting the Irish economy get out of control. As a country, we were boastful of our economic success in going from one of Europe's poorer countries to one of the richest. But where is that wealth now? It was stolen away from us through agreements made between us and the EU, which obliged us to support the banks that had failed. How could we turn around and say 'no' to the EU when we had become so dependent on them for trade and investment?

Our predicament reminds me of what John prophesied about the Church in Laodicia:

> "You say, 'I am rich; I have acquired wealth and do not need a thing.' But you do not realise that you are wretched, pitiful, poor, blind and naked." [Revelation 3:17 NIV]

Our reliance for what we need as individuals, and also as a country, should be on God and not on those who tempt us with cheap credit. Surely we cannot look back at the Protestant Ascendancy and say anything in judgement of them when our generation have done something much worse! Furthermore we cannot hope to repent for the past sins until we ourselves repent for the financial gain that we sought during the boom. Let us cast our memory back to the fact that the EU initially didn't want us to join! They turned down our first application with several of the member states referring to Ireland's neutrality during World War II as a basis for their decision. We cannot blame the Irish government either, as on 10th May 1972 the Irish people voted (83%) in favour of joining the EU. Our membership was signed into law on the 8th of June 1972 at a ceremony held at Áras an Uachtaráin. In doing so we signed away certain rights and dependencies which should have been ascribed to God. This is because:

- God's law should take precedence over our national laws. Instead, after 1972 EU law took precedence over Irish law.
- Our dependency should remain on God so that we look to Him for solutions to our problems. Instead, joining the EU was seen to be the answer to problems of high emigration and high unemployment. Thus our dependency on Europe began and continued to grow.

This is not to say that God didn't want us to join the EU. He might have but, if He did want us to join, He would have wanted it to be done according to His standards. One of the 'yes' promotional posters of the time stated, "The balance favours entry" and portrayed scales comparing reasons to join with reasons not to join. Yet, the poster was worded in a way that all of the reasons really pointed to a 'yes' vote. Many of the reasons cited were based on the fear of "What if we don't join and continue to experience high unemployment and high immigration?" Fear is not a good reason for doing anything! Yet, it is quite often underlies modern advertising, especially when insurance companies want people to imagine the worst that might happen to their property. This is contrary to how a Holy Spirit filled person thinks and reacts. The Word of God teaches us to be strong and courageous [Deuteronomy 31:6], that we can do all things through Christ [Philippians 4:13]. It helps us not to fear because God is with us [Isaiah 41:10] and shows us that if we love God then all things will work out for good [Romans 8:28]. Our main priority, therefore, is to love God and trust Him to look after us. We need not fear any of the things that people of the world fear because Christ resides in our hearts and He holds everything under His control. The 'yes' campaign for Europe was led by those who stated that it was morally right and proper for Ireland to do so. However, this meant that 'righteousness' had been replaced by 'moral correctness'. The serious outcome of doing so is seen in Romans 10:

> "Since they did not know the righteousness of God and sought to establish their own, they did not submit to God's righteousness." [Romans 10:3 NIV]

Those who voted 'yes' were perhaps following the example of previous Irish leaders who themselves had been tarnished. Éamon de Valera, the president in 1972, had had a long political career which had begun during Ireland's struggle for Independence. He was one of the leaders captured after the 1916 Rising who had not been executed. In 1926, he and some other politicians formed Fianna Fáil, the political party that would eventually lead Ireland into the boom and bust period of our recent time. It seems to me that he and his party were proud of what they had done for Ireland. Perhaps he felt that he had played a prominent role in the fight to win Irish Independence and was proud of what he had achieved. Also Áras an Uachtaráin, his official residence during his presidency, had links going back to the Protestant Ascendancy as it was built in 1780s and, under British rule, was known the Viceregal Lodge.

Jesus taught how leaders should act. He certainly did not encourage them to rebel against God or to have pride in their hearts over anything that's achieved through their leadership. He pointed to Himself as the example of 'servant-leadership':

> "Jesus called them together and said, "You know that those who are regarded as rulers of the Gentiles lord it over them, and their high officials exercise authority over them. Not so with you. Instead, whoever wants to become great among you must be your servant, and whoever wants to be first must be slave of all. For even the Son of Man did not come to be served, but to serve, and to give his life as a ransom for many." [Mark 10:42-45 NIV]

I have seen this wrong kind of leadership in the lives of so many people. They talk about how they founded their particular ministry. They may even have it as a title for themselves on their website or *Facebook* page referring to them as the 'founder' of their work. In truth, we have no right to make such claims if we believe God had anything to do with it. It is either God who founded the work or man who founded it. If it was founded by God then it will have God-given results. If it was founded by men, it will have humanistic results. Jesus warned that if a man has found favour and reward in the eyes of men, then he has already received his reward [Matthew 6]. However, I want to receive a heavenly reward! I want to engage in ministry that God has founded. I want to be part of the church that Jesus is building. Here are principles showing, generally speaking, how a ministry should develop. It is important to understand these things so that we are not deceived:

1. Step one: God has a plan.
2. Step two: God puts this plan on a person's heart. It might be the heart of an intercessor or the heart of a prophet. God tells him or her to go to a certain place and pray/prophesy about a future ministry there. It may not be one person but hundreds or even thousands who come together to ask God for it in response to hearing His directive.
3. Step three: God answers the prayers of the intercessors/prophets.
4. Step four: God calls a person with the necessary anointing (and mantle) to establish the ministry that has already been prayed and prophesied about. For example, a pastor may come into an area to establish a church there. This could happen immediately after step two or maybe five, ten or even a hundred years later.
5. Step five: The ministry leader (e.g. the pastor) must continually seek God to ensure that the ordained path is followed. On the other hand, he may help to develop others who can listen and follow God's plan for the ministry there to set him free to move on to other areas.

Now tell me, would it be right for a pastor, such as the one referred to above, to say that he founded the ministry? His role is just a subordinate one that may have come about following hundreds of years of prayer and also preparations made by God. If God founded it, then

God is the founder of it. Pride is very much linked to false claims such as those which we covered in an earlier chapter. We saw it in people like Wolfe Tone who falsely claimed to the King of France that the whole of Ireland was united in rebellion. Paul wrote to the Galatian believers about the results of such pride:

> "If anyone thinks they are something when they are not, they deceive themselves." [Galatians 6:3 NIV]

According to this train of thought, we should avoid anyone who lays claims to have founded anything for they have either become proud, or have laid foundations of something which will manifest pride later on. Such pride and self-centredness is forbidden is Scripture:

> "Do nothing out of selfish ambition or vain conceit. Rather, in humility value others above yourselves, not looking to your own interests but each of you to the interests of the others." [Philippians 2:3-4 NIV]

So Edith and I came to understand that our primary prayer target would need to be Áras an Uachtaráin because we would have to repent for the present generation before we could proceed to repent for earlier ones. We made plans and went along to the Visitor Centre in the Phoenix Park on a Saturday morning so that we could join one of the guided tours around the Áras. It wasn't a place that either of us had been to before and we struggled to find parking. However, we managed to get in the door just a minute before the buses were leaving to bring people up to the Áras.

The guided tours leave from the Visitor Centre by bus and it takes about an hour to complete the tour. We got into the bus and it drove off. Soon we were at the big white gates of the Áras. The gates looked old but they opened automatically. A guard came out to check us before the bus moved on. As we drove on we saw lines of trees with plaques placed in front of them. Obviously, these trees had been planted during visits by important people. We pulled up at the rear of the house, which is absolutely huge. Some other people joined our group and we headed inside after being informed that we could not take any photos inside the building. Just before we entered, I read out this verse:

> "We demolish arguments and every pretension that sets itself up against the knowledge of God, and we take captive every thought to make it obedient to Christ." [2 Corinthians 10:5 NIV]

The first place they brought us to was where the President's car was stored. We saw a car there that was most famously used by Éamon de Valera during his presidency. There are current plans to re-install the engine and use this car once again.

Photos: the President's car and the garden at Áras an Uachtaráin

My first impressions were of opulence and pride. This was something I witnessed right throughout the house. So, as we walked through it, we prayed and repented of the specific things that God had called us there to repent of: the decisions made through pride. We were then led up to the state rooms which is where the official ceremonies and receptions take place. Every one of these rooms was adorned with distinguished sculptures, paintings, carpets and furniture. However, there was a sinister spiritual element in evidence there. We couldn't help but notice the symbolic and idolatrous nature of some of the objects on display, most notably in two places, the state room and the president's office.

On the floor of the state room was a huge hand-made rug that had been made in Donegal in 2000. The design was based upon a previous one dating from the 1950's. The rug portrayed four river gods and in the centre was a mythical bird called a phoenix which was rising from the ashes. While the other visitors seemed to be awed by the skill and vastness of the design, I was disgusted that such an idolatrous piece of work was allowed a place in the room where many of the affairs of the state are conducted.

The four river god design traces its origin back to sculptures made for the Custom House by the Irish sculptor Edward Smyth. The Custom House in fact has fourteen of these river gods relating to the main rivers of Ireland. Each sculpture has its own symbology and intricate design but the meaning is about a god who controls the flow, the peace and turbulence of the river and also takes responsibility for the land covered and the fruit born from the waters. Edward Smyth also carved two figures that are to be seen on the south portico of the Custom House. They were named 'plenty' and 'industry' reflecting the wealth that gained a foothold in our land. Surely, these physical things display the spiritual influence on decisions made in that room.

The phoenix depicted at the centre of the rug is something that is shameful to have on a rug in one of our state buildings. This idea of the phoenix rising from the ashes was the same imagery used by the republican campaign that began in 1969. The slogan used at the time was, "Out of the ashes rose the Provisional IRA." How this symbology ended up on this rug I do not know but I do know that, according to Romans 13, rebellion against authority is the equivalent of rebellion against God. So, in the centre of the rug is a reminder of the rebellion that this country has taken against God. Not just as with the IRA in recent time, but all the way back in history to the earliest of rebellions that took place.

The second idolatrous image that really concerned me was on the ceiling of the President's study. Here we saw a design depicting 'The Elements and Seasons being presided over by Jupiter'. Jupiter was a sky-god in Roman mythology and his role was to act as a witness to oath-making which was believed to be essential to justice and good government. In Roman times, politicians were sworn into office by the name of Jupiter. Later on they would be required to offer sacrifices to him. I knew that we were not called to come here to pray about such things but we did pray to ask God to raise up a president who would have the wisdom and power to remove these symbols of idolatry just as King Hezekiah did when he came to power [2 Kings 18:4]. On the way back to the Visitors' Centre, God gave me a scripture referring to what was going on. So, after we left, we pulled up our car outside the gates of the Áras and prayed prayers based on the following scripture:

> "During the reign of King Josiah, the Lord said to me, "Have you seen what faithless Israel has done? She has gone up on every high hill and under every spreading tree and has committed adultery there. I thought that after she had done all this she would return to me but she did not, and her unfaithful sister Judah saw it. I gave faithless Israel her certificate of divorce and sent her away because of all her adulteries. Yet I saw that her unfaithful sister Judah had no fear; she also went out and committed adultery. Because Israel's immorality mattered so little to her, she defiled the land and committed adultery with stone and wood. In spite of all this, her unfaithful sister Judah did not return to me with all her heart, but only in pretence," declares the Lord. The Lord said to me, "Faithless Israel is more righteous than unfaithful Judah. Go, proclaim this message toward the north: " 'Return, faithless Israel,' declares the Lord, 'I will frown on you no longer, for I am faithful,' declares the Lord, 'I will not be angry forever. Only acknowledge your guilt— you have rebelled against the Lord your God, you have scattered your favours to foreign gods under every spreading tree, and have not obeyed me,' " declares the Lord. "Return, faithless

people," declares the Lord, "for I am your husband. I will choose you—one from a town and two from a clan—and bring you to Zion. Then I will give you shepherds after my own heart, who will lead you with knowledge and understanding. In those days, when your numbers have increased greatly in the land," declares the Lord, "people will no longer say, 'The ark of the covenant of the Lord.' It will never enter their minds or be remembered; it will not be missed, nor will another one be made. At that time they will call Jerusalem The Throne of the Lord, and all nations will gather in Jerusalem to honour the name of the Lord. No longer will they follow the stubbornness of their evil hearts. In those days the people of Judah will join the people of Israel, and together they will come from a northern land to the land I gave your ancestors as an inheritance. "I myself said, " 'How gladly would I treat you like my children and give you a pleasant land, the most beautiful inheritance of any nation.' I thought you would call me 'Father' and not turn away from following me. But like a woman unfaithful to her husband, so you, Israel, have been unfaithful to me," declares the Lord. A cry is heard on the barren heights, the weeping and pleading of the people of Israel, because they have perverted their ways and have forgotten the Lord their God. "Return, faithless people; I will cure you of backsliding." "Yes, we will come to you, for you are the Lord our God. Surely the idolatrous commotion on the hills and mountains is a deception; surely in the Lord our God is the salvation of Israel. From our youth shameful gods have consumed the fruits of our ancestors' labour— their flocks and herds, their sons and daughters. Let us lie down in our shame, and let our disgrace cover us. We have sinned against the Lord our God, both we and our ancestors; from our youth till this day we have not obeyed the Lord our God." [Jeremiah 3:6-25 NIV]

The next day Edith and I travelled by coach up to Belfast. From there we travelled by bus, getting off at the stop nearest to Belfast Castle.

The sky was clear and it was a lovely fresh spring day as we began to walk to the castle. First, we went into the Visitor Centre at the Castle and left our heavy bags there so that we would not have to climb all the way to the top of the hill carrying them. We had brought luggage in order to have a change of clothes because we were due to attend a book-launch later that evening of a book entitled *Seeds for the Journey*[19].

Photos: the caves(top) and the view from half-way up(bottom)

As we walked up through the forest, we tried our best to walk at a quick pace to make sure that we would be able to spend some time at the top and be to get back down before the Visitor Centre closed. As we climbed, I wondered why the men might have specifically come here to Cavehill to climb to the top. I pictured their determination and resolve playing a part and also the assurance that there weren't any attendees there who were not willing to put in an effort. Cavehill rises to 1200ft above sea-level, not as high as Church Mountain, but nevertheless walking up the steep parts of the hill was still quite a challenge. In some areas, there is a cliff edge right beside the path and so it's not a place for people with a fear of heights. About half-way up we came across some man-made caves but we moved on past them without stopping, eager to get to the top.

As the ground began to level off, we prayed for the strength to continue on and soon we were at the top. We began to ask God to show us where He wanted us to pray. There were some people up there playing loud music and we asked God to 'change the atmosphere' for us and, after we prayed, they moved off. Then God brought us to one particular spot and I felt a nudge to stop there and pray. We hadn't gone quite as far as McArt's fort but it was very near to us and can be seen in the image below. When I stopped, I looked down and there at my feet was a rock with a large crack running along it. As I put my hand to it, it fell apart and I brought a piece of it back with me to put it with the stones from the other locations that we had already visited. Then God gave me these Scripture verses:

> "They delight the king with their wickedness, the princes with their lies. They are all adulterers, burning like an oven whose fire the baker need not stir from the kneading of the dough till it rises. On the day of the festival of our king the princes become inflamed with wine, and he joins hands with the mockers. Their hearts are like an oven; they approach him with intrigue. Their passion smoulders all night; in the morning it blazes like a flaming fire. All of them are hot as an oven; they devour their rulers. All their kings fall, and none of them calls on me."

[Hosea 7:3-7 NIV]

Photo: view from the top of Cavehill

I believe that God was showing us that the gathering here by Wolfe Tone and others was done by people with fiery hearts filled with frustration or even anger about the state of Ireland at that time. Instead of turning to God, they fed their own fury. It was just as the above verses say, "None of them calls on me." Then we prayed and repented for them. As we did, a refreshing breeze came over the hill and refreshed our bodies. Edith began to prophesy that there would be a 'spiritual stirring' in Belfast and that a refreshing wind would blow its way across the city. This verse came flooding back to us. It was the one that we had discussed as we travelled up to Belfast:

"Whoever believes in me, as Scripture has said, rivers of living water will flow from within them." [John 7:38 NIV]

Later that day, we had further confirmation of this when we arrived at the previously mentioned book-launch. There we learnt that, as part of the programme, they wanted me to read out one of the poems in the book. I said yes straightaway but when I saw the title of the poem I laughed out loud. It was called 'He pours' and it brought me straight back to verse above and made me think once again about the importance what Jesus taught about living water.

Chapter Fourteen
An outpouring of humility

God knows our hearts. That is a simple fact which so many of us easily forget and we carry on through life as if God can't see us. We imagine that God doesn't mind if we watch such and such a movie or that God doesn't mind whether or not we pray tonight or if we arrange a meeting and exert our control over it. The truth is that God is always with us and sees absolutely everything that we do or say. The only reason why we might want to think otherwise is to satisfy the desires of our humanity! In fact, we as humans often make assumptions that aren't true. For example, we might think that attending church makes us a Christian or that bringing our children to Sunday school makes them Christians. We might convince ourselves that the pastor in our church can't make any mistakes or that the sermons we hear on Sundays reflect a theology that is 100% true. We could also assume that the people who serve at church do so with a 'good heart'. To think like this is dangerous. We have to be realistic and get rid of assumptions like these if we are to see clearly how pride gets in and affects the church.

A good example of where pride can cause problems is in connection with worship leaders. We look at them from the congregation and think "Wow! These people are so talented in their music and are so humble because they are dedicating their time and energy to their ministry".

However, this assumption could be far from the truth. They may indeed appear to be humble, but in reality they might be full of pride. In my opinion, if an ounce of pride exists in anyone involved in leading the worship time, they should either step down or be removed. I believe that we should no longer accept or promote pride in our brothers and sisters. To do this we need to stop sharing videos and photos of them on our social networks as these tend to encourage them in the wrong manner by telling them how great they are. It is God who has created gifts in these people, so only God should receive the glory for it.

What we need in all our churches today is an outpouring of humility and every proud person brought to his or her knees and every humble person respected. In the Kingdom of God, those who are humble have first place. Jesus, our Saviour and example, humbled himself time and time again. We are nothing and we have nothing except what Jesus has given to us. We must understand that pride is at the core of the religious heart and we must not tolerate it in any shape or form, whether in our own hearts or in the lives of our church leaders. I am not saying that we put people out of the church, but that we correct them in love and in the right manner as set out in the Word of God. This is important, if a proud person remains in leadership, then they will be likely to attract other people who will have pride in their hearts too.

Remember what we learned from our history. One group of people can be suppressed while another group gets into a position of dominance over them. Those on top are often the ones filled with pride while those underneath are the ones who are humble. The problem with pride is that it is not just the responsibility of those who display it; the blame is also on the people who fill them with pride by their praise. Those who are humble are often quiet and slow to speak. Many of them feel that they are not in a position to challenge people with pride in their hearts. Every person in the church should have the right to rebuke or correct any other person in that church as long as it is done in love. If that person is unsure how to go about this, they can seek guidance from a godly elder or trusted mentor, especially if he or she is a new believer. However, generally speaking, this is not how modern churches operate. Leaders often stand on 'pedestals' that the people in their churches have created for them. They expect their leaders to make no mistakes and so, if a leader does make a mistake, which is common to us all as human beings, then they have to cover it up. There is a better train of thought based on power achieved through humility rather than through pride. David Wilkerson, made this principle clear at a conference entitled *'The Hope that purifies'*[17]. You can tell by the way he taught that he understood the power of being humble and admitting mistakes. Instead of 'preaching', he shared with the pastors who had gathered his own frailty and mistakes and even about how he had once lost the anointing of God. That, my brothers and sisters, was more powerful than any theological sermon could be. The key is humility. We really need an outpouring of it in all our churches. David Wilkerson, through his honesty, was able to really challenge the hearts of each of those pastors and to help them regain the anointing of God in their lives. A theological sermon could never have achieved that same level of impact. I believe that David Wilkerson found the same sort of strength as Paul, who wrote about how God strengthened him in his weakness:

> "But he (God) said to me, "My grace is sufficient for you, for my power is made perfect in weakness." There I will boast all the more gladly about my weaknesses, so that Christ's power may rest on me." [2 Corinthians 12:9]

Will God listen to a person with a heart filled with pride who prays aloud about wretched people living on the streets? Or will God listen to the man crying out for the same people but, instead of being proud, he recognises that he himself is wretched in the sight of God. God has regard for those who are humble and therefore may completely refuse to answer the prayer of a person who has a heart filled with pride. The challenge for us is one of discernment as only God can see the state of a person's heart. Jesus taught us the following principle that helps us to know what a person's heart is like:

> "A good man brings good things out of the good stored up in his heart, and an evil man brings evil things out of the evil stored up in his heart. For the mouth speaks what the heart is full of." [Luke 6:45 NIV]

If the mouth speaks of what the heart is full of, then all that we need to do is listen to what people are saying. If they are saying how good they are and regularly speak of what they have achieved, then that gives us an insight as to what is the condition of their hearts. If, however, they admit their frailties and their mistakes, then that admission goes a long way to show that there is humility in their hearts. Once you have discerned who has a heart of pride and who does not, then you must be careful of the words that you allow to reach your own heart. Secondly, it is better not to judge such people but pray for them that they may become more humble. If there is a preacher that you previously listened to on the internet but now know to have pride in his heart, then do not listen to him anymore. If the preacher is someone in your church, then you need to seek God about what to do about him. The difficulty often is that a person with a heart full of pride will not take rebuke or correction easily. They may not respond at all and may even ostracise you. They may even shout at you or say bad things about you behind your back. Therefore, always use caution when confronting proud people. You don't know whether the whole purpose of the pride instigated by the enemy is to cause issues in the church or even bring about a church split and you might fall prey to his trap by unwisely opening your mouth concerning the issue. In such circumstances, we must always follow what God tells us do to and not depend on our own understanding. James gave guidelines that will help us deal with such issues in a proper fashion:

> "My dear brothers and sisters, take note of this: Everyone should be quick to listen, slow to speak and slow to become angry," [James 1:19 NIV]

Another thing to realise is that pride leads to the telling of lies and a false sense of reality. It is as if it creates a kind of bubble in which people then exist. They only accept things that support their position and turn aside from everything else. They can sometimes even use selected passages from the Word of God to justify what they do or what they say. If, however, those people were to stand before Jesus seated on His throne in all His majesty, they would realise how wretched they really are. In fact, their bubble would disintegrate! I have drawn a diagram to illustrate what often happens in churches when a person is proudly in position at the centre of his or her bubble:

If people were to live like this, it would be very difficult for them to hold on to humility in their hearts. I am not saying that people who are well known in Christian circles can't remain humble but that we as their brothers and sisters in Christ must do all that we can not to inflate them or their position any more than it should be. We must not boast about any preacher but instead boast of Jesus Christ and of all that He has done and is doing in our lives. The person that you meet on the street doesn't want to hear about some famous preacher from half-way across the world. However, if you share your testimony with them, then they will be more likely to respond. We need to keep in mind that nobody will achieve a knowledge of God that is 100% proof whilst here on this earth. It is impossible for any person to understand the vastness of God. As a result, we should be careful not to promote any preacher and describe him to others as a great teacher. What if his doctrine later changes and becomes heretical? Then you may have advised someone to blindly follow that teacher and fill his mind with what he says. Our dependence must be on God and on God alone. It is okay to depend on your pastor temporarily if you are a new believer as he will help to train and equip you. Later on, when maturity comes, dependency on your pastor needs to drastically decrease or even cease altogether. Instead you will by then have grown to be able to stand side by side with him, or to even be a pastor yourself, if that is your calling.

Our dependency on God, of course, needs to be in place for all aspects of our lives and, not just church-life. For examples of this we can look back at the history of Ireland to see what happened when we didn't place our trust in God but instead trusted in the EU for jobs and so many other things. As Christian believers, we have to be honest and ask are we living a life that is separated from the world. So many Christians follow exactly the same life-path as non-believers and go to school when aged 4-5 years until they are aged 17-18, then on to college or university until they are 21-25 years. Then get a job and so on. That has become the stereotyped life of the modern Irish person. But, what if God wanted us to do things differently? Have we ever asked Him? Have we checked with Him, for example, how He wants us to raise our children? Are we aware of the idolatry and false teachings that are rife within our schools? Essentially, we put our children into classrooms for non-believers to teach them. We may think, "Oh, it's just maths and history, etcetera. It has nothing to do with God!" Do not forget that

God has something to say about everything that we decide or do. To not seek His leading is foolish as we leave ourselves open to sin. If our children spend most of their schooldays learning from non-believers, how can we claim that we are bringing them up in the way of the Lord? Are they not just being brought up in the way of the world? I am not saying that we must remove our children from the schools, but we should at least seek God for guidance and not just simply send our children to school because the 'world' tells us this is the correct thing to do.

Ignoring God's guidance is something that is very much linked to our pride. We think, "It's okay. I can handle this decision on my own." Remember the example of Wolfe Tone. He tried to do something in his own strength, in his case to unite the Catholics and the Protestants. It just didn't work! Often, in churches, we find people doing exactly the same thing – trying to do things in their own strength. Every single activity that you can imagine in a church's programme is susceptible to this and so we must always proceed with caution. Being 'mature in Christ' does not infer that we no longer need to depend on others because we are strong. Instead, maturity in Christ means that we recognise our weakness and, because of them, hold on to Christ with a tight grasp, knowing that we are nothing without Him.

Another thing to bear in mind is that if we put our dependence on anyone or anything other than God, then those things become our gods. Jeremiah said that when we give our trust over to other gods then they will consume the fruits of our labour [Jeremiah 3:22-24]. If the foundation for decisions made at Áras an Uachtaráin is given over to the gods of plenty and the gods of industry, then it is those same gods who will consume the fruit of all that we get from our labour. Joining the EU is a prime example. We gained jobs and money only to have those jobs and money stripped away from us by the very same people who once helped us. If we put our reliance on anything but God then in time, the people and things we trusted will end up bringing us harm. Irish history also showed us that rebellion only ruined what hope we had and served to make everything worse. Are we any more confident now about the future of our nation's financial prospects because we are an EU member when we see the current troubled state of the EU's finances?

However, God is always gracious. If we turn to Him and repent of our ways then we will find that God has not given up on Ireland. We need to respond to the warnings given in Scripture such as this one in the Book of Revelation:

> "You say, 'I am rich; I have acquired wealth and do not need a thing.' But you do not realise that you are wretched, pitiful, poor, blind and naked." [Revelation 3:17 NIV]

Perhaps you remember this verse quoted in the last chapter. In my view it is important to properly understand this verse as our pride is linked directly to our dependence. If we are dependent on our wealth then we cannot at the same time be dependent on God! Let's look closer at the meanings of some of the words from this passage:

- 'Wretched' basically means being extremely unhappy. How often do we see famous people in the world who have reached such a level of unhappiness that they abuse themselves with drugs or, even worse, commit suicide? Why do so many people crave fame when those who achieve it are so often unhappy? Fame does not ensure happiness.
- 'Pitiful' besides meaning 'to be pitied' this word can also mean inadequate. If you look closely at famous people, you'll often see that they often consider themselves to be inadequate. For example, you will find them spending money to adjust their appearances as they age through the use of plastic surgery in an attempt to enhance how they look. You will also find many famous people using names that are not their real names. It seems very difficult for them to 'be who they really are'.
- 'Poor' is often used in terms of money, but it can also mean an inferior standard, similar in meaning to the previous point. Fame demands having standards that famous people have to constantly live up to. It might involve them going to the extreme measure of having plastic surgery or it might mean that

they can't step outside their own homes without having their makeup on or that they can't walk down the street in their pyjamas when they want to.
- 'Blind' means lacking visual perception or awareness. God opposes the proud and this means that He is not there to lead a person who is filled with pride. As a result, they must make their decisions in life without access to the guidance of God.
- 'Naked' means undisguised and exposed. How many famous people are able to go on their holidays without finding pictures of themselves in their swimwear in the papers the next day? How often are candid photos taken by ex-partners and then 'leaked' on to the internet? Their fame has only served to bring into their lives a global desire, where others want to see them exposed. It requires constant vigilance by these people in order to protect themselves from such exposure.

Our wretched state cannot be hidden from God, we are told in Hebrews that one day we will have to give account for everything:

> "Nothing in all creation is hidden from God's sight. Everything is uncovered and laid bare before the eyes of him to whom we must give account." [Hebrews 4:13 NIV]

You see, pride is not a bubble that floats us into some happy place. It's a bubble that's at the surface of a lake but when weights are added (slowly or quickly) they pull the bubble under until there is nothing left. This is why the Book of Revelation describes elders around the throne in heaven taking off their crowns and laying them at the feet of Jesus. They are removing any weight and attitude of pride and giving all the glory to Jesus. In practice, pride is a huge weight to carry. Imagine not being able to express what is on your heart. We saw this symbolised on our visit to Áras an Uachtaráin when no photographs of the interior of the house were allowed to be taken. In a similar way, we are prevented from seeing the truth about what is on the inside of a proud heart. We cannot see it but we know that it is detestable to God. It makes me think of when we were walking along that ridge on the way up to

Cavehill. One slip and we would have a long way to fall!

The other things that we noticed in Áras an Uachtaráin were the historic objects set in place so that they could not be removed. Likewise, it is difficult for a famous person to become 'un-famous', to reverse the things that they did that made them famous in the first place. Those things are carried with them, just as Áras an Uachtaráin is full of objects that have been collected over the years since the forming of our nation. The President is not allowed to remove these objects even if he wants to! If a famous and proud person tries to 'disappear off the radar' because they find that their bubble is sinking, they will find it very hard to remain incognito. Similarly, a proud church leader who wishes to humble himself will find it very difficult to do so.

Ironically, pride does however give people the desire to hide from God. But, their hiding is like that of the little boy who hid under his bed to escape from an imaginary attacker. In reality, therefore, how safe are these people in their hiding place? They try to hide from God; they shy away from His glory and ignore His calls to turn from their sinful ways but they cannot hide forever under their 'bed'. Proud people never want to admit their pride. They push the truth away from them because the truth is too much for them to face. Instead, their bubble seems the ideal place for them to stay in. That is, until it sinks. Hiding from God is always associated with fear. Consider Adam and Eve who hid in fear of God's presence in the garden. They did not want God to discover what they had done.

In closing, let us summarise what we should do about pride and proud people:

- We must ensure that pride is excluded from the lives of believers so that the atmosphere in our churches is changed for the better.
- We need to refresh the church with a new strength or energy through allowing God to create an outpouring of humility
- We need to put our dependency back on God and God alone

The truth is that our churches have been infiltrated by the 'yeast of the

Pharisees', and so we must throw it all out and start over again. Imagine for a moment that you are alive back in the time just after Jesus' crucifixion. Where do you turn for the answers for what to do? Our focus should be on God so that He can guide us on each and every step. We all claim to be disciples of Jesus when we call ourselves a Christian.

So be that disciple!

Chapter Fifteen
Religion starved us
A barren place, Dublin Mountains

Research has shown that Ireland suffered over fifty famines since the time of Jesus' birth[11]. Famine, as Moses warned the people in his day, forms part of the curse for people who do not obey God:

> "You will sow much seed in the field but you will harvest little, because locusts will devour it. You will plant vineyards and cultivate them but you will not drink the wine or gather the grapes, because worms will eat them. You will have olive trees throughout your country but you will not use the oil, because the olives will drop off. You will have sons and daughters but you will not keep them, because they will go into captivity. Swarms of locusts will take over all your trees and the crops of your land." [Deuteronomy 28:38-42 NIV]

What I found very interesting when researching famines in Ireland was the variety of reasons why they occurred in our land. I think that each of these reasons has a spiritual significance that God wants us to reflect on and so, in this chapter, we will go through some of those events and examine their spiritual meaning.

Today in Ireland we don't need to worry about food. We just go down to our local supermarket and food is always there and always available. The supply of food in Ireland has been reasonably stable since the late 19th century with imports from other countries helping to keep our shelves stocked all year round. We can even buy fruit and vegetables out of season because they are imported from other places around the world. Imports currently account for about 12% of the food on our shelves but, back in the 1960s, we imported as much as 20%. However, before this time of plenty, there were several famines in this country. We are all probably aware of at least the potato famine that happened in the middle of the 19th century. In the Bible as we have already seen, God warns that famine will result when people rebel against Him. Ezekiel prophesied that when God's judgement came, the results would be inescapable:

> "Son of man, if a country sins against me by being unfaithful and I stretch out my hand against it to cut off its food supply and send famine upon it and kill its people and their animals..." [Ezekiel 14:13 NIV]

When we look back at our history there were so many times when famine occurred without any recorded reason. Examples of these were A.D. 664, 759, 824-825, 1153, 1227, 1294-96, 1302, 1314-6, 1331, 1339, 1410, 1433, 1447, 1497, 1522, 1741, 1831 and 1879.

Even though no physical reasons were recorded explaining why these famines occurred, we can be sure that there were spiritual reasons. We should remember the love of God and remind ourselves that it is not His will that any should perish. To allow a famine to arrive in a land would therefore be the last thing that God would do in response to a nation's rebellion against Him. But when famine happens, they are often very drastic. In recent times we have seen in the media images of countries that have been in a famine. These images were shocking and yet, just a hundred and fifty years ago, the Irish people were in the same situation. However, it has been so long since we had famine in Ireland that my generation has heard very little about it except in history class in school. In a way, all of this does not make sense. If anything, our modern society has moved even further from God, so why aren't we experiencing famine now? While there have been times when bad weather disrupted crops and harvesting and measurable changes to climate patterns, these changes have not been enough to bring famine to the land. However, I believe that after so many tragedies in our land that when God saw that we were hardening our hearts even further He gave us over to something even worse than physical famine. He allowed us to descend into a spiritual famine. This is in keeping with what He warned through the prophet Amos:

> "The days are coming," declares the Sovereign Lord, "when I will send a famine through the land— not a famine of food or a thirst for water, but a famine of hearing the words of the Lord." [Amos 8:11 NIV]

Many people have read this verse and interpreted it as envisaging a time in history when people will be unable to purchase a Bible. Instead, I see it as a time when people no longer know how to hear for themselves what God is saying, leaving thousands and thousands of 'believers' totally dependent on their church leaders for guidance. Even many of the leaders do not know how to listen for God or else they would surely be teaching the people who attend their churches. Surely then, that time of spiritual famine is now upon us. How often do you come to a church and hear people share what they have heard God telling them? But, however, I am certain that God has not forgotten us because I know that He has been active in the last few years restoring prophetic gifts in people so that they can hear from God once again. Sadly, many of those prophetic voices have been disregarded or even excommunicated from their churches for claiming that they hear from God. Does this mean that we, as a nation, are happy with being starved spiritually?

A poor or failed harvest brings famine

In Irish history it was the failure of the harvests that brought famine on our land. This was true of the famines during A.D. 10-15, 192, 1727-29 and 1822. When we look at how the church has performed over the past hundred and fifty years, we could also say that we have had failed spiritual crops. In the so-called evangelical churches, generations have come and gone but the church has not expanded by any great amount because we are losing 88% of the rising generation to the enemy[6]. In other denominations, attendance at church was more about culture, a portrayal of a fashionable way of life. Over the years, we have developed our teaching, our philosophy, our sermons, our music but none of these have brought us as close to God as those people who have sought God in such depth that revival was awakened. There are many popular books that tell the story of such men and women of God. The books might be popular, but when will the people in churches do what these men and women of God have done before us, and seek God with all our hearts?

When we lose a spiritual harvest is has a devastating effect. Parents may watch their children leave home and live the worst kinds of lifestyle without having the power to do anything about it. Evangelists also may face a failed harvest. They may focus more on getting people to say a quick prayer rather than seeing them experience true salvation and discipleship. Their spiritual crops may shine for a little while then wilt and fade away, because the hearts of the people they reached never truly left the world.

We need to be honest with ourselves about these things. If 88% of the children in our church families are lost to the enemy, let's admit it and seek God for help to change it. If our evangelism is dry and not Holy Spirit led then let's admit that too and seek God for guidance how to change it to ways that are more productive. This is urgent and we need to find the answer before the next crop fails. We really have to! It's a fight for our very survival. Those who never hear the message of salvation and those who walk away from it are dying in their sin. We are somehow content to let these people pass us by, but, if our son or daughter came and told us that they have cancer, how much more would we be on our knees before God seeking His help? Is sin a lesser disease? No, sin is far, far worse than cancer because it brings death to the eternal soul. Only those who have accepted Jesus as their Saviour will be saved. The change starts with you, and starts with me. How willing are we to seek God?

A lack of food supply brings famine

In Ireland there have been times where the scarcity of food brought famine. Examples of these famines occurred in A.D. 76, 669-670, 1188, 1765 and 1812. The Bible also gives the reason why God allows such things to happen:

> "He then said to me: "Son of man, I am about to cut off the food supply in Jerusalem. The people will eat rationed food in anxiety and drink rationed water in despair, for food and water will be scarce. They will be appalled at the sight of each other and will waste away because of their sin." [Ezekiel 4:16-17 NIV]

The spiritual significance of this is easy to see. In our churches today we may have from five to perhaps ten people who seem to be filled with spiritual food and overflowing with Spirit-given gifts while everyone else may be showing very little spiritual growth and some may even be starving to death, spiritually speaking. The majority may be disheartened, seeing others with plenty while they have very little. Tragically, all of this can happen despite the promise that Jesus gave us when He said:

> "I am the bread of life. Whoever comes to me will never go hungry, and whoever believes in me will never be thirsty." [John 6:35]

So, what is wrong that causes people go to church and yet go home spiritually hungry? The answer lies in what we do at church. I had a vision a couple of years ago of many thirsty people going out to seek water. They all went to a local well and drank from it but there was never enough water to meet all of their needs. Meanwhile, just nearby was a well that had an unlimited supply but sadly no one went there. The people had actually forgotten where it was and had become so caught up in their routine that they never stopped to consider that there might be access to a better source of water. This taught me that there is an unending vastness of revelation and love available from God and we need to come and receive it from Him. There is a well of Living Water and when we drink from it, it will become a well of Living Water springing up inside us [John 4:14].

Extreme worldwide events bring famine

We have mentioned before the extreme weather conditions back in the 6th century that brought darkness across the whole earth. In Ireland, the impact of this on the people caused many to search for God in a deeper way and as a result many became true believers. We have to remember that Ireland is a small country and events that happen beyond our shores are very much out of our control. However, everything in the world is under God's control. A major global disaster has not happened in recent time, although there have been several large scale natural disasters such as the 2004 tsunami in the Far East. But these events seem insignificant when compared to things that the human race endured in history and also may endure in the future. Some TV programmes and movies describe disasters that could befall us. To take one example, Yellowstone National Park in the United States which was recently discovered to be a huge active volcano. If it were to erupt, it could cause a worldwide volcanic winter, and many parts of America would be utterly devastated.

However frightening such things may sound, it is true to say that, if we believe in God and trust Him then there is no need to fear any of these events. If we survive them, then God has sustained us and if we perish, then God has taken us home. The most important thing is to live according to God's will. I remember hearing an intercessor at Bible school teaching us about when she went into an active war-zone. She knew that God had asked her to go and held to her faith in God even when huddled down in a bomb-shelter as missiles hit the city. She told us that it was better to have been in a dangerous place in God's will than to have been in a safe place but not in God's will. Think about this statement for a moment. We don't actually know how many times God has saved us from harm. He may have diverted someone, who otherwise would have crashed into our car, to take another route to work, thus saving us. Recently, I was going on to the motorway and while on the on-ramp, the driver in front of me stopped suddenly instead of merging with traffic. I saw what was happening in time and stopped but another car came around the bend behind me at speed and the driver had to make an emergency stop and I braced myself for the impact. However, before all of this, I had prayed and asked God to help me get to work safely. The car didn't hit mine in spite of the skidding and swerving. I'm sure that it was God's angels that brought him to a halt. It made me wonder how many times God has saved us from danger. If He saves us, then why should we fear things like volcanoes? The Lord will look after us provided that we know Jesus, and that we love and obey Him.

Disease and cannibalism during famine

Several times in our history during famines cannibalism was reported such as during the famines that occurred in A.D. 700, 1116, 1262, 1271, 1601-1603 and 1690. It is shocking to think that people could be so desperate that they would be willing to kill others and eat them or to eat the rotting flesh of those who had already died. In some cases parents even ate their own children's flesh! When I originally read Deuteronomy 28 and read about people resorting to cannibalism, I said to myself, "There is no way that such a thing could have happened here." I had thought the same when I read about slavery – that it could never happen here either but I was wrong. These things have tragically been part of our history and such extremes, as said above, were recorded in the Bible. Jeremiah prophesised that cannibalism would be part of God's judgement against the people of Judah and Jerusalem:

> "I will make them eat the flesh of their sons and daughters, and they will eat one another's flesh because their enemies will press the siege so hard against them to destroy them.'"
> [Jeremiah 19:9 NIV]

Sometimes where cannibalism was reported, the outbreak of disease was also reported as rampant. We have seen in modern history that, when people weakened by the from lack of food, disease can spread rapidly such as when dysentery reached epidemic proportions during a later famine that took place in 1847. Disease could also have other effects as when farmers caught diseases and died and so obviously could no longer farm the land thus further reducing availability of food. Indeed some famines had disease as their primary cause.

Spiritually speaking, we have already discussed the issue of disease and shown how false religion spread and infected the people. It spread quickly. Jesus warned about the 'dough of the Pharisees'. The corruption caused by this kind of religion in our hearts can very easily be expressed and destroy our brothers and sisters in Christ. We can, for example, mock them on social networks, gossip about them or, even worse openly speak negatively against them. To me, these things are acts of spiritual cannibalism because we are willing to feed on the demise of others in order to further our own ends. This is contrary to the principles on which the kingdom of God is built. Instead, it's the kingdom of the enemy that is built upon such things. Our Christian duty is to love our brothers and sisters, even to the extent of laying down our lives to protect them. If they fail we are to correct them in a godly manner, and support them with a heart of love. Let us bring to an end our spiritual acts of cannibalism. Let us repent from doing things our way and instead follow the way God has ordained. Remember, it is He who, by His grace and mercy, has cover over our sins by the blood of Jesus Christ.

Earthquake and famine

There was actually one time in Irish history where an earthquake occurred simultaneously with a famine. This was in A.D. 768. Isaiah prophesied such events in his prophecy against Babylon:

> "Therefore I will make the heavens tremble; and the earth will shake from its place at the wrath of the Lord Almighty, in the day of his burning anger." [Isaiah 13:13 NIV]

People often attribute extreme events that happen in nature to be acts of God, such as being struck by lightning or being devastated by an earthquake. The verse above shows how Isaiah saw earthquakes as being the 'wrath of the Lord Almighty.' A more recent example of this was the Great Earthquake of California which occurred on the 18th of April 1906, and resulted in three-thousand people being killed and 80% of San Francisco being destroyed. However, at ground level, God was moving. A Christian believer circulated leaflets claiming that the earthquake had been the result of the judgement of God on the city. This challenge was followed by an outpouring of the Holy Spirit. The spiritual revival is now known as the Azusa Street revival so having got its name from the location of the central church involved.

Today it is difficult for us to know what was happening at ground level here in Ireland back in 768 when this earthquake and associated famine occurred. It may well have been a warning from God because of the manifestation of power struggles in the churches of the day. It could also have been a 'warning shot' before the Viking invasions were unleashed upon us! God in His mercy gives us opportunities to turn from our sinful ways, because, as stated above, He does not want anyone to perish. But He warns us that if we persist in our sin, a day will come when we will stand before Him and be judged. As well as facing judgement in the next life, we can also receive judgement while here on earth. This is because God's law states that there always will be consequences for our sinful actions.

Spiritually speaking, during the earthquake, God was shaking things up. We know that the majority of earthquakes or tremors recorded in Ireland in modern times are small and mostly ignored. However, God can shake things up in a small way or in a big way. If we keep ignoring His shaking, then the shaking will get worse. During the last four years (2010-2014) we have actually had forty-three earthquakes, more than what we had during the previous twenty years! They have grown both in number and intensity. I believe that this is because if reflects the reality that God is also shaking things up spiritually. As a result, many of us have been shaken out of our comfort zones during the last four years. But this is not disastrous. I believe that God is doing this in order to position us for what lies ahead in the future.

He shakes us up in order to move us on to the next point in our learning and relationship with Him. If we refuse to move on, then we will become stuck in a position of spiritual famine which will remain until the Lord comes and shakes us up completely. I have seen this happen with individuals and also with churches. The Lord is never content for us to remain in a one place, caught in a kind of spiritual doldrum. He desires our lives to be a continual journey. We go through different seasons but we have to recognise these seasons or we will be prevented from moving forwards. My conclusion is, if God is shaking you up, allow Him to do it! He will bring you to a place of peace on the other side, a place that is lined up for you and included with your future in Him.

Drought caused famine

It is a strange thing to think of Ireland having had a drought when we have such a wet climate but a drought actually did lead to famine in A.D. 772. Drought is something that is referred to in the Bible, showing that the land can get to such a point where there is no water and where fires ravage the pastures as a result. It also describes the cattle moaning because the extent of their thirst. Both Joel and Haggai prophesied that famines such as these would take place:

> "You expected much, but see, it turned out to be little. What you brought home, I blew away. Why?" declares the Lord Almighty. "Because of my house, which remains a ruin, while each of you is busy with your own house. Therefore, because of you the heavens have withheld their dew and the earth its crops. I called for a drought on the fields and the mountains, on the grain, the new wine, the olive oil and everything else the ground produces, on people and livestock, and on all the labour of your hands." [Haggai 1:9-11 NIV]

> "The seeds are shrivelled beneath the clods. The storehouses are in ruins, the granaries have been broken down, for the grain has dried up. How the cattle moan! The herds mill about because they have no pasture; even the flocks of sheep are suffering. To you, Lord, I call, for fire has devoured the pastures

in the wilderness and flames have burned up all the trees of the field. Even the wild animals pant for you; the streams of water have dried up and fire has devoured the pastures in the wilderness." [Joel 1:17-20 NIV]

The significant thing that God is teaching us is that, spiritually speaking, we have dried up. Our hearts have become hardened and our eyes no longer shed tears. We may attend church but we merely exist as believers, going through the motions without growth or maturity. This is a spiritual famine and it is caused by a lack of an outpouring of God's Spirit. The wells have become blocked and must be unblocked in order for the outpouring to begin again. Remember Jesus' promise in John's Gospel about the coming gift of the Holy Spirit:

"Whoever believes in me, as Scripture has said, rivers of living water will flow from within them." [John 7:38 NIV]

You may ask what is the living water that is to pour from you and me? I see it as love, produced by the indwelling Holy Spirit. This love produces fruit that is born out of God's love and out of no other source. The river of God as described in the Bible [Ezekiel 47, Revelation 22] has trees planted along each side that bear fruit and have leaves that are for healing. This living water is supposed to flow through us on a constant basis. It is not our living water; it is the living water that comes from God and produces an overflow of love, pouring itself out on to anyone who encounters us. How often have you spent time with another believer and come away having felt the love of God in him or her? How often have you experienced such love at church? The challenge to ask ourselves, "Are we bearing fruit that is based on the love of God or our meetings 'dry events' that produce no fruit other than mere attendance?

The verse quoted above from Haggai says that the Lord brought drought on the land because his house remained a ruin. Instead of looking after God's house, they were focussed on their own homes. That was of course took place in the Old Testament. We are now living under the new covenant and this means that the house of God is now our hearts.

What condition are our hearts in? Do our hearts lie in ruins, unrepaired from damage? We need to let the Lord re-build our hearts so that what was damaged can be replaced by His structures. We need to have fully restored hearts so that God can make our hearts His home. Take my own life for example. I suffered some severe emotional distress as a child and it damaged my heart. Today, I could be a Christian and yet still allow that damage to remain. On the other hand, I can hand it all over to God so that He can make all things in me brand new. When God's house (i.e. our hearts) is repaired or in the process of being repaired, then His love pours into our hearts and transforms our lives. That is when the spiritual drought ends!

Locusts caused famine

Once again we find some amazing events that happened during our history. In A.D. 895-897 it was reported that swarms of locusts had brought famine to Ireland. Locusts are simply swarming grasshoppers. The scientists say that a chemical called serotonin in their brains triggers the condition that makes them swarm. You might ask who triggers the release of serotonin. The Bible attributes the swarms of locusts that plagued Egypt to the power of God's words spoken in judgement:

> "He spoke, and the locusts came, grasshoppers without number; they ate up every green thing in their land, ate up the produce of their soil." [Psalm 105:34-35 NIV]

When swarms of locusts came across the land and devoured the crops there was very little that the farmers could do, especially before the use of pesticides and other chemicals. There was of course one consolation. The locusts themselves could be eaten and would have been quite high in protein. The verses above from the Psalms describe what had happened when Moses was challenging Pharaoh to let the Israelites go free. In that way, it was not an attack on God's people but upon their enemies. The ninth century in Ireland was very much influenced by the Vikings and perhaps the famine at that time was sent to weaken the Viking hold on Ireland. It is significant that soon after this, in 902, the 'heathens' were finally driven out of Ireland.

So what is all of this saying to us about where we are today spiritually? I think it is showing us that God is willing to allow famine to come to areas of Ireland where the enemy has been prevailing to give us a window of opportunity to drive the enemy out of the land. I believe that God can certainly stop the enemy in his tracks just as He did in the time of Isaiah where He announced to the King of Assyria:

> "Because you rage against me and because your insolence has reached my ears, I will put my hook in your nose and my bit in your mouth, and I will make you return by the way you came."
> [Isaiah 37:29 NIV]

Cold weather caused famine

Those of us who have the privilege of living in Ireland know that when a relatively small amount of snow falls the whole nation can grind to a halt. We are blessed with a temperate climate and not used to snow. However, in our history there were records of cold weather that was so severe that it destroyed crops and brought famine. This happened in particular in A.D. 1047, 1200 and 1739.

I believe that spiritual famine can come as a result of being cold-hearted. When someone is filled with love, it is evident what kind of heart he or she has. This is also true for those who are cold-hearted. I'm not referring to murderers and the like. I am talking about doing good things like helping the needy, the homeless, the widows or the orphans. It is true that we can do these things from other motives. Indeed, non-believers may do volunteer work and even run charities dedicated to helping people. We don't know what the motives of the heart are but God does. He will reward those who do their good deeds out of love for Him. Speaking about Himself as King, Jesus said:

> "The King will reply, 'Truly I tell you, whatever you did for one of the least of these brothers and sisters of mine, you did for me."
> [Matthew 25:40]

You see, we should not help people so that we can proudly count our good deeds. Nor should we do them because it is our duty to do so.

We should do them because we have come to love God so much that we love to do what He loves to do. God has not forgotten the beggars, the orphans and the widows. He loves each of them dearly. When we understand his love for them and that He never gives up on them, then we begin to understand how we should respond. In the above verse quoted from Matthew, we are told that what we did for the least of those that Jesus called 'brothers and sisters', we actually did for Him. Therefore, if we have fed the homeless, we have fed Jesus. If we took in an orphan into our family then we have taken Jesus into our family. Tragically, if we haven't done these things then the opposite is true. We might be asked for money by a beggar but give Jesus nothing. We might see an orphan who needs a home but now allow Jesus to join our family. We might see a widow being evicted from her home but did not welcome Jesus to come and live in our home.

I had a vision a while back about a man who took in a homeless person, but that homeless person robbed him and ran away. The lesson I learned was that we must not take grudges to heart for what people do to us nor for how they may waste opportunities. Jesus told us to give to the one who asks from us and if someone asks us to go with them for a mile, then we are to go two miles with them [Matthew 5:41-42]. I used to be quite reluctant to offer people lifts home or to other places. That was until I met my wife Edith who has a wonderful ministry of giving lifts, often offering to drive people home even to distant places at her expense. Her willingness amazed me and God used it to help me improve on showing love to others in practical ways. I have learned that our hands should never have a closed fist but instead have open palms. God fills our hands, but He may also send along people who will help themselves to what He gave us. He does this so that they can come to know God through what we share with them. So, let us not be cold-hearted to others or to God. Instead, let us learn to be more loving in all that we do.

War caused famine

There were of course several times when Ireland was at war and armies burnt the crops as they moved across the land. The effects of war caused famines in A.D. 1317-18, 1582-1589 and 1650-1651. These famines were self-inflicted. Sometimes, even those doing the burning ended up starving later on. In a way burning crops makes no sense. Why burn up badly needed resources? Why burn up what was needed for sustenance? Of course, the armies involved were trying to prevent their enemies from having access to the crops. But then, nobody had the use of them. Rather than taking the food for themselves, they preferred to burn the whole lot so no one could get them. It reminds me of the story of King Solomon and the baby he ordered to be cut in two. The bereaved mother agreed that the baby should be killed so that neither she nor the other mother would have a child. It was because of her reaction, that God gave Solomon the wisdom to know which mother the child belonged to.

This story gives us an insight into what happened in Irish History. Certainly, in 1650, the famine was caused by English soldiers burning the land. What does this tell us? It tells us that England, like the mother who would rather have the baby cut in two, did not own the land. It was the right of the Irish people to have and to possess the land. This is a reminder of one of God's plans for Ireland that we all need to recognise but I admit that it is a very complex situation. Having possibly already offended all Republicans by what I have written in this book, I now find that this journey will take us to discuss issues which might also offend Unionists. However, at the end of the day, it is true to say that human opinion varies hugely. This is in contrast to God's will. As God, He does not succumb to the wish of man unless it agrees with His will. People may quote verses from the Bible out of context and use them to argue their case. However, even if they do this until they are blue in the face, they still cannot change what God thinks. Our proposal is not to put the Republicans and the Unionists into the same room and get them to debate together and work out some form of agreement. Rather, it is for both sides to come together before God to learn what He has to say to them. To make progress in this area, we must be willing, to drop our own particular cause and instead take up God's cause and do what pleases Him.

Blight caused famine

When most people talk about famine in Ireland, they refer to the Great Famine that began in 1845 and continued for several years. Blight is something very specific on the list of curses that God puts on those who are not listening to Him and are not walking in His ways. Blight is essentially a disease that rots a plant. The potato blight hit Ireland at a time when the Irish were heavily dependent on potatoes for food. Our population was decimated during this famine with many hundreds dying from starvation or disease and thousands of others leaving for foreign countries never to return.

What this says to us spiritually is that our spiritual crop or our spiritual harvest is rotting away. If you take a healthy plant and put it into a place that is infected, it too will become infected. Even if you filled the land with several thousand plants, all of them would be infected. Remember how we saw that false religion is like a disease. Our spiritual crops have become infested by the disease of such religion. If we take brand new healthy plants (i.e. new believers) and put them into situations where they only experience religion, they will absorb that religion, the disease. Thereby potential for future harvest is lost. Instead of us raising up disciples of Jesus Christ we raise up believers who are spiritually blighted.

What is the solution? We need to develop a system (a field) that is free from disease (false religion). That is what this journey that Edith and I are making is about. The only way we can get rid of blight is to pull up the diseased plants by the roots and remove them from the ground. In the same way, God has been pulling up diseased plants (blighted by the religious roots of the past) so that they can be removed from the garden (Ireland). We now need to look to the future. We need to anticipate a disease free harvest, with disease-free plants bearing much fruit.

During famines we exchanged our possessions for food

Imagine for a moment, that you went down to your local supermarket and they didn't have enough food and the people had queued up outside in order to try and get their basic necessities. You queued up as well but it took you three hours to get some food and get to the checkout. There you discovered that the price of food had risen dramatically and the few items you managed to get from the poorly stocked shelves would cost you four hundred euro. You paid but immediately started to worry about the next day's food. You went home and got together all your spare money. By the next day your money was all spent and so, by the third day, you have no money left. How soon would it be before you started to sell your possessions? Your TV, your jewellery, your furniture, everything's gets sold off in exchange for food. None of those material things are important because the need for food comes first. In the famine that took place back in 963-964, parents even traded their children for food. Similar desperate measures are also recorded in the Bible:

> "All her people groan as they search for bread; they barter their treasures for food to keep themselves alive. "Look, Lord, and consider, for I am despised." [Lamentations 1:11 NIV]

Now, instead of seeing yourself in a physical famine, imagine you are in the middle of a spiritual famine. You do all that you can to get sustenance from the Lord but instead everything seems empty. What would you be willing to sell or to give up, in order to receive the food you need to keep yourself from starving? Despite spiritual starvation, we have seen little movement of people who will forsake the infertile famine-ridden land of dead religion and instead come into the Lord's land, the land where His promises are fulfilled.

During famine we abandoned our own rules

It is to be expected that when the Irish people were hungry and thirsty that they would start to 'abandon ship', as it were, and begin to disobey the laws of the country. People would now steal food or even kill other people and take their food. In one famine it was recorded that priests even gave up the rules for Lent so that they could eat the meat that was available. This actually happened in 1203. However, when we look at other famines such as the Great Famine, people abandoned their families and their loved ones and emigrated to America or to other countries in order to find food. They went where there was the hope of food. The same kind of thing will happen in a spiritual famine. People will leave the system that brought them into the famine in the hope that they will find what they need from the Lord. The time for this is now upon us here in Ireland. We are a people known for emigration but now we must become known for our spiritual migration, away from dead religion and back to God. In fact, we leave nothing behind that is of value. We move on to a future hope, trusting that God as our Shepherd will bring us to green pastures.

Seeking the face of the Lord

I had known for maybe a couple of years that a day would come when I would have to go up a mountain by myself and seek the face of the Lord. It was during my research that I stumbled across this verse:

> "During the reign of David, there was a famine for three successive years; so David sought the face of the Lord. The Lord said, "It is on account of Saul and his blood-stained house; it is because he put the Gibeonites to death." [2 Samuel 21:1 NIV]

When David sought the Lord for an answer concerning the famine that had struck his land for three successive years, God gave him a specific answer. I knew that this was what I must do, to seek the face of the Lord on a mountain in order to find out the reason why we have been in a spiritual famine in this country for such a long time. God called me to come and seek Him in a 'barren place'.

Photo: view of the Dublin Mountains

I drove up into the mountains near my home and parked the car. God began to speak to me. These are the words He said:

"Go to a barren place and hear me. Come up, come up to the mountains and hear my voice. My voice, it drifts across the barren mountain like a strong wind. For Jesus has come, the Stem of Jesse, the Righteous Judge!"

I remembered words written in prophecy by Isaiah:

> "The infant will play near the cobra's den, and the young child will put its hand into the viper's nest. They will neither harm nor destroy on all my holy mountain, for the earth will be filled with the knowledge of the Lord as the waters cover the sea. In that day the Root of Jesse will stand as a banner for the peoples; the nations will rally to him, and his resting place will be glorious." [Isaiah 11:8-10 NIV]

God continued speaking to me.

"You have stood under my protection. The vipers have snapped at your heels but you did not faint. The snakes invaded your home but you chased them without fear. But now my son, look at the snake that was with you all along. It's the one that has kept you in this barren place, the place of starvation and harshness. Here, there are no crops. Here, there are no trees that bear fruit. Grain will not grow here. Even the people flee from its wind. Look at the other mountains and see the stony places where falling rocks can kill a man, where thunder can strike a sheep to death. Do you see any joy? Do you witness any relief?"

"Now look my son at your own barren heart. Look back at the places where you starved, they are but the roots of things planted in this place. Is it okay that you should plant here? In the wanderings of your man-made ideas? No! Tell me which direction is the Promised Land from here? Tell me, where can you plant a seed so that it will grow in this place? I tell you that not even one thing that you plant in your religion will grow! Therefore pull them out from your heart, all your desperation, all your grand ideas, all your ministry aspirations and see the truth. You

are nothing yet you mean everything to me. Look yonder and tell me what you see."

I looked and saw the water of a lake and farms down below in the valley and I spoke about these to Him.

"Just as you have spoken, I shall bring you to my Valley where you shall walk amongst the farms and see many crops. Why stay here where there is barrenness? Just let me lead you."

"Have your way, Lord; but turn my heart into your path," I prayed.

"Never again come to this barren place. It's a place where rotten things are discarded, where the unwanted things are left, where people fight over what little there is, fighting here amongst the rocks. Never come here to plant. Never come here to find a crop or you shall reap nothing as in the days of your forefathers. Never chase the wind."

This time a quotation from Ecclesiastes came to me:

> "A person can do nothing better than to eat and drink and find satisfaction in their own toil. This too, I see, is from the hand of God, for without him, who can eat or find enjoyment? To the person who pleases him, God gives wisdom, knowledge and happiness, but to the sinner he gives the task of gathering and storing up wealth to hand it over to the one who pleases God. This too is meaningless, a chasing after the wind." [Ecclesiastes 2:24-26 NIV]

"Now go down into the Valley of the Lord. Wash your hands, wash your face. Prepare to do my work and not your own. Wash your hands so that they do not carry the stain of your own works, but be clean to do my will. Wash your face so that you do not display your own works but let it be cleansed so I can shine upon it and reveal my glory."

Photo: view of valley and Dublin in the distance

I turned to the Book of Ezekiel and read the following:

> "I will sprinkle clean water on you, and you will be clean; I will cleanse you from all your impurities and from all your idols. I will give you a new heart and put a new spirit in you; I will remove from you your heart of stone and give you a heart of flesh. And I will put my Spirit in you and move you to follow my decrees and be careful to keep my laws. Then you will live in the land I gave your ancestors; you will be my people, and I will be your God. I will save you from all your uncleanness. I will call for the grain and make it plentiful and will not bring famine upon you. I will increase the fruit of the trees and the crops of the field, so that you will no longer suffer disgrace among the nations because of famine." [Ezekiel 36:25-30 NIV]

Chapter Sixteen
A heart of stone
Hill of Uisneach, County Westmeath

One morning God woke me up and asked me to go walking with Him and so I did. While I walked He said this to me, "Two you know of, and one remains hidden". Now the two that I knew about were pride and starvation. At that time I still had not taken the trips related to those two things and the last piece of the puzzle had, until this point, been hidden from me. I began to seek God about where the last location of the religious roots were buried. Eventually, I was led to read about a place called 'The Hill of Uisneach'. I don't know about other Irish people who grew up in Ireland but I had never heard of this place before. The more I read about it, the more astounded I became.

The Hill of Uisneach is located not far from Athlone and, to this day it remains, a place of prime spiritual importance. In our ancient past, Uisneach was believed to be the centre of Ireland and indeed it was located where the original five provinces met. Some people believe that because of its location Uisneach is the place on Ptolemy's map called Raiba because of its location. Legend tells us that, when the Milesians came to conquer the Ireland and its people, at the time, Ireland was ruled by the Tuatha Dé Danann. As the invaders approached Uisneach, where King Dagda had his throne, three sisters came out to meet with them and to negotiate peace. After the meeting, it was decided to name the island after one of the sisters. Her name was Ériu which in the Irish language of today is pronounced Éire.

The legends give this information but I believe that there is a piece missing from this story as I have come to believe that the three sisters were actually the daughters of King Dagda. The Milesian king had come to take the land. It was a personal matter in order to avenge the death of his son who had been killed by the Danaans. It would make sense then that, if one of the daughters were to be killed, the debt would be paid and peace could exist between the two groups. It is known that peace did occur but the record of the death of one of the sisters has been erased from history. One can almost visualise them making the agreement and announcing, "The debt is paid. Let's leave a marker of peace here at the very centre of the country to remind us."

The only record states that she was buried underneath 'The Catstone'. The most significant thing at Uisneach for me, is this Catstone, the large rock feature that is said to weigh about 30 tonnes and stands almost six metres high. Underneath this rock Ériu is said to have been buried. The Catstone got its name from the people who first saw it thought that it resembled the shape of a cat pouncing on a mouse. However, it is also known as 'The Navel' of Ireland, or as 'The Heart-stone' of Ireland. That a Heart-stone of Ireland actually exists is very significant, especially in view of the fact that we have been on this journey. In the last chapter I shared about how God promised to give us a new heart, adding that we would no longer have a heart of stone. That refers, not only to us as individuals, but also to Ireland as a nation.

After those ancient events, pagan rituals began to take place at Uisneach, including the Beltane Festival which was held on the first of May. At this festival, people used fire to help protect themselves from evil spirits and sacrifices were made to gods such as Beil. Indeed, even Ériu was made into a goddess. Notice the similarities between Beil and Baal, a god that we recognise from Bible times. The following quotation records reforms made by King Josiah after he came to power in Jerusalem:

> "He did away with the idolatrous priests appointed by the kings of Judah to burn incense on the high places of the towns of Judah and on those around Jerusalem—those who burned incense to Baal, to the sun and moon, to the constellations and to all the starry hosts." [2 Kings 23:5 NIV]

It is no coincidence that the two names are the same. Most students of this period of history identify the god worshipped in the Festival as Baal. Indeed, the very same rituals are still carried out in the West Indies where the festival is called 'Belton'. However, the old ritual of killing babies is no longer practiced but the traces of it have stayed behind, charred bones were uncovered by modern archaeology at Uisneach. In the West Indies, it is believed that the devil himself presided over the festivities. Uisneach was also a central location for politics, for manmade religion and indeed even for devil-worship. Uisneach today has no political influence anymore yet a spiritual significance remains that is recognised by all who know about its existence. From the top of the hill, you can see as many as twenty counties of Ireland on a clear day. I think this is simply astonishing! It is no mere coincidence therefore that this place which overlooks so much of the Irish countryside Ireland is also the very centre of corrupt religion.

Uisneach was not only steeped in paganism, but also in Christianity. It is believed that Saint Patrick came here and there is a well on the site named after him. I know that in many other locations erroneous claims were made that said, "Patrick came here". However, I can believe it's the truth about this place because it was the centre of paganism in Patrick's day. Not only that but, when I visited the official website for the Uisneach site, it claimed that this was the location where the 1111 synod took place when the decision was made to divide Ireland up into dioceses. When I had researched those four synods, I had gone to Cashel to pray there as the first synod had been held there in 1101. Since then, the question of where the other hidden synod had taken place had lingered on in my mind. Now, at last, I had the answer.

Non-religious events have also taken place at Uisneach. For example, in 1919, Eamon de Valera addressed a Sinn Féin rally at the hill and, in 1691, William of Orange's army travelled past Uisneach on their way to fight the armies of James II. Further back, in 999, Brian Boru came to Uisneach to claim kingship over the Kingdom of Meath. This site therefore, not only lies at the spiritual centre of paganism but it also has the spiritual roots of a religiousness that has Christianity woven into it, intermingled with the various historic events.

The thing that I find to be most significant is that the heart-stone of Ireland is actually a real stone. That may sound like a silly statement to make but we have been on a journey about religiousness and here at the centre of it all is a heart of stone. In the same way, at the centre of our own religiousness, we too have a heart of stone. Note the references to hardness in the following three quotations from the New Testament:

> "Do not harden your hearts as you did in the rebellion, during the time of testing in the wilderness" [Hebrews 3:8 NIV]
>
> "For this people's heart has become calloused; they hardly hear with their ears, and they have closed their eyes. Otherwise they might see with their eyes, hear with their ears, understand with their hearts and turn, and I would heal them.'" [Matthew 13:15 NIV]
>
> "They are darkened in their understanding and separated from the life of God because of the ignorance that is in them due to the hardening of their hearts." [Ephesians 4:18 NIV]

Once again, God was going to reveal how his hand had been guiding us. I had planned to head to Uisneach one Saturday but, however some family visitors turned up and I had to postpone it until the next day. On Sunday morning we went to church first. While there, I asked God to give me a verse that was for Uisneach and the Holy Spirit told me to turn to Isaiah 17:3 which reads:

> "The fortified city will disappear from Ephraim, and royal power from Damascus; the remnant of Aram will be like the glory of the Israelites," declares the Lord Almighty." [Isaiah 17:3 NIV]

I think that, normally speaking, this is one of those verses that you come across in the Bible and merely skim over. However, I prayed and asked God for some more insight so that I could better understand its significance. I ended up reading another verse that He led me to. It gave me the understanding about deliverance that I needed to learn:

> "A prophecy: The word of the Lord is against the land of Hadrach and will come to rest on Damascus— for the eyes of all people and all the tribes of Israel are on the Lord —" [Zechariah 9:1 NIV]

From this latter verse, I came to understand that when the eyes of the people are on the Lord, then God's words wreak judgement on their enemies. Damascus was the capital of Syria and certainly represented King David's enemies. He had fought them and eventually had placed military outposts in their lands. Understanding this, on the way to Uisneach after church, we re-visited the previous verse from Isaiah in order to get a better understanding of it. First we looked at the name 'Ephraim' which means 'one who is fruitful in the land of affliction'. When we thought back to the history of Joseph in Egypt, we saw that he certainly was fruitful after the affliction of being in prison. But his name was also prophetic showing that the land of Egypt would be a place of affliction and that the Israelites living there would face hundreds of years of slavery after the death of Joseph. Yet, in spite of their enslavement, the Israelites they did multiply whilst there and when they left for the Promised Land, they also took with them the riches of Egypt. So we interpreted the verse as relevant to the ending of spiritual enslavement in Ireland, showing that the affliction of the land of Ireland will disappear and that the power of the enemy will also disappear. These points helped us to work out the meaning of the rest of the verse. Our discoveries were as follows:

- Aram was the area known today as Syria. It was said to be the place where Noah's eldest son Shem settled after the flood.
- Jesus also helped Syrians during His ministry in Galilee and surrounding areas [Matthew4:24].
- The name 'Aram' comes from the Hebrew word 'ram' which means height, lofty stature, pride or haughtiness.
- There were three people in the Bible named Ram and one of them was an ancestor of King David and therefore also of Jesus.
- The 'remnant' of course refers to the people who are left because they turned to God when the larger part of the people had either been removed or destroyed.

We saw that the 'remnant of Aram' then surely refers to those who would turn to God for deliverance. Indeed, the 'glory of the Israelites' was the fact that their God was with them and His presence went before them. The same would also be true for the remnant. God would be with them and walk amongst them. It reminded us of the vision of John in the Book of Revelation:

> "And I heard a loud voice from the throne saying, "Look! God's dwelling place is now among the people, and he will dwell with them. They will be his people, and God himself will be with them and be their God." [Revelation 21:3 NIV]

When Edith and I arrived at Uisneach, we found some parking nearby and approached the gate. At the gate we found that a sign had been put up which said "Strictly No Access." I knew that the following weekend was to be the Bealtaine Festival and realised that they were probably busy with the preparations for it. Undeterred, we noticed that there was a party of sorts going on in a nearby house; they even had a bouncy castle up for the children. We walked over, introduced ourselves and asked them about Uisneach and if anyone there knew how we could somehow get permission to go inside the site. One woman went into the house and returned with a man who turned out to be the owner of the farm land on which Uisneach sits. We explained the reason for our visit to him but we could see that he was a bit frustrated by our arrival and would probably be unwilling to supervise us due to the fact that he was attending the party. He went off to make a couple of phone calls and while he was doing this; we prayed and stood in faith that God would help us. He returned and told us that we could enter as a man who was working for him just happened to be present on the farm.

We thanked him but, as we walked away, we thanked God even more and entered through the gate. Once again, God had given us an entry where no entry was allowed. We walked up a long lane and prayed to God, asking Him to keep bad weather at bay, which He did. At the top of the lane we found a small hut and also met the man that the farmer had told us about. He gave us a quick run-down of the site and started going into the history and also the idolatry. He spoke about the pagan gods as if the worship of them was something mystical. It became clear to us that the place still carried with it a mysticism that made people think great things of things which were not. For me, I see people like Ériu as real people who became idolised after their deaths. The people made Ériu into a goddess just like the people later on also made Patrick into an idol.

Photo: the King's house

We went up on to the location of the palace of the kings and stood there. We noticed a small ring of stones with a larger stone in the centre (pictured above). From this vantage point where two houses had once stood and where the King of the Danaans had built his house, you can see the ancient road that led in one direction to Cashel and in the other to Tara. Some historians claim that the Danaans were actually descendants of the tribe of Dan who survived the Assyrian captivity and eventually came to Ireland and settled here. It is impossible to know for sure if such things did happen but it did come to my mind briefly as I stood there at this ancient place.

The tombs around this site date back to around 5000 B.C. showing that this place has been a centre of activity since the very beginning of Ireland as a nation. One of these tombs had been demolished and then reassembled to form what is now known as 'Saint Patrick's bed'. It is found at the very summit of Uisneach. I recalled that Patrick also had a bed named after him on top of Croagh Patrick. The local people there at Uisneach told us the legend of when Patrick had come to Uisneach. They said that he had come here after Tara and set up a church on top of the hill. At that time two brothers were occupying the local kingships and they had argued between them whether Patrick could stay or not. One supported Patrick but the other did not but, in the end, they decided to banish Patrick from the hill. As he left, he put a curse on the stones saying that they would be brittle and that no one would come there to use them anymore. Right near where we were standing, a large bonfire was under construction for the upcoming pagan festival. Seeing it, we prayed and asked God to return our land into the hands of His people so that paganism can be banished forever and Patrick's mission made complete.

Photos: view from St Patrick's bed (top), tree coming out of a rock (left) and small lake (right)

I have to say that the whole area around Uisneach, although containing many things of interest, has a strange feel to it. There is a variety of ancient structures to which people in recent times have added pieces of artwork, such as carved images of gods. Each one of these modern additions depicts objects of worship that are detestable in the sight of God Almighty. Also in the area, there is a small lake where one of the 'gods' met his mortal fate when his brother drowned him. Once again, I say that these were probably actual people who were later made into 'gods' by people with religious minds. There was also a strange looking tree that seemed to be growing out of a rock. There were also several other strange looking trees on that hill.

We walked down the other side of the hill and located the Catstone. All around it, a wire fence had been erected which was obviously designed to keep festival-goers away from it. The Catstone looks small in photos but it is actually very big, and with the way that the rocks are placed on top of one another, it looks quite unstable. I certainly would not risk climbing on top of it. I went under the fence and walked carefully around the Catstone and prayed. Underneath it I found a small piece which had fallen off and I took it with me. Edith and I prayed together asking God to remove our hard hearts, to break our heart of stone so that we may change our ways and love Him passionately, both as individual people and as a nation.

Photo: the Catstone

Chapter Seventeen
Reconciliation

Letters of Reconciliation

During this journey for God, I had recognised very early on that the time would come when I would need to write letters to those who lived outside our country but yet had considerable influence on what happened inside our country. Even though the people I am referring to are no longer alive, their authority structure still exists. Their representatives included the Pope, the Queen Elizabeth II and the British government. The letters will not reach the actual people who did us wrong but we can still send them a message of forgiveness on behalf of the people of Ireland. The importance of forgiveness is certainly emphasised in the Bible and is made clear in the following passages from the pen of Saint Paul:

> "Bless those who persecute you; bless and do not curse."
> [Romans 12:14 NIV]

> "Bear with each other and forgive one another if any of you has a grievance against someone. Forgive as the Lord forgave you."
> [Colossians 3:13 NIV]

> "Therefore, if anyone is in Christ, the new creation has come: The old has gone, the new is here! All this is from God, who

reconciled us to himself through Christ and gave us the ministry of reconciliation: that God was reconciling the world to himself in Christ, not counting people's sins against them. And he has committed to us the message of reconciliation." [2 Corinthians 5:17-19 NIV]

I believe that we must forgive all those who persecuted the Irish people, and also all of the Irish people who made wrong decisions during our history. This is something personal that each Irish person needs to do in his or her heart. Forgiveness means letting go. Forgiveness entails not speaking ill of the perpetrators again as we once did. For example, I have forgiven Oliver Cromwell. As a result, I can't go back anymore and speak in anger about all that he did while on his campaigns here in Ireland. I can't hold on to anger against England or the Pope. I have found that holding on to grudges is not a godly thing to do! God clearly stated in His Word that if we judge others then we too shall be judged. We have found in this journey how we the Irish people made many wrong choices and brought curses upon ourselves. Nobody else was responsible for bringing them here. As we look to the future, we must remember these facts and actively fear the Lord God and follow His guidance. If our country decides to go in the wrong direction then we need to be actively praying and repenting for our fellow countrymen.

Photo: posting of the letters

The removal of the stones

As you have seen, during this journey God was teaching me along the way during this journey about removing the stones. We now have collected twelve stones from the following places that we visited:

1 stone from Church Mountain,

3 stones from Kilashee, Kilcullen & Domnach Sechnaill,

1 stone from Drumcliff,

1 stone from the Rock of Cashel,

1 stone from Clonmacnoise,

2 stones from Dublin & Galway beaches,

1 stone from Cavehill,

1 stone from Uisneach,

and 1 stone from Dublin Mountains.

The revelation about collecting these stones and removing them led us into a gradual learning process. At the beginning, I did not fully understand why we had to do it but we had certainly learnt why by the time we finished. Soon afterwards, God spoke to me and told me that we would have to take the ferry across to Wales. A short while later, two friends of ours, Rose and Kevin Sambrook informed us about 'Part-2' of a set of conferences entitled "The Gathering of the Clans" that was to be held in Wales on the first weekend in May. As soon as I had heard this, I knew that this would be the right time to travel on the ferry and to cast away the stones into the deep waters of the Irish Sea.

However as it got closer to the time, some difficulties arose but, however, everything that needed to happen in order to get away fell into place for us in an amazing way. We knew that God was with us. Financially, we had seen God's provision for us all along the way covering everything we needed for this journey. Simultaneously, we had been learning about this provision as part of our preparations for our wedding that was to take place that July. Indeed, we received so much favour in each of these things that we will always look back fondly at these six months of our lives. However, when the time came to book our ferry tickets, we found that it wasn't as easy as before to get the money together. Nor was the timeline working out easily for us as neither of us could get any more time off work in order to attend something like a conference. We delayed our decision but eventually, we came to understand that we would just have to take a step of faith, trusting that God would restore to us the cost of travel. Also, seeing that we would be travelling for eleven or twelve hours each way and only be able to attend two of the conference sessions, we would have to do this in faith, trusting that God would keep us strong. We plucked up courage and booked the tickets.

Leaving on the Friday the 1st of May, we caught the 2:15am ferry and began the long ferry-rail journey from Dublin to Swansea. I fell asleep and it must have been about half three when the Holy Spirit woke me from my sleep. I took out the bag of stones from my luggage and went up on deck where I faced a harsh wind and spray coming up from the sea. I walked along the deck until I got to a place where I could easily throw the stones into the water. In the distance I could just about make out the lights along the Irish shoreline. I opened the bag and I prayed over each stone as I cast them down into the water below. I knew that I was not to just drop them but instead to cast them into the water. To drop something infers that it was done by mistake. There was no mistake in this task, however. God had sent us to do this, and we had answered His call.

I may have been half asleep at the time, but I thanked God that He was leading me even as we completed this one last task. Edith had stayed patiently by our luggage, praying while I was out on deck. She was my companion on this journey and she was also the second witness to each of these events. With only a few short weeks left before our wedding day, we had learnt so much about how to support each other as we moved forward into whatever God was leading us to do.

At the conference, God began to speak to us again. At the evening session, the speaker, Ray Hughes, delivered a very powerful message about spiritual famine and finished at the point where Elisha prophesied that 'this time tomorrow things will change' [2 Kings 7:1]. Now, we could see that something dramatic was going to happen on this last night, the Sunday night, which would signal the anointing for those who would march forth into a spiritually famine-struck land and cause it to prosper. We realised that, just as the conference would be finishing, we would be on the ferry heading back to Ireland, to claim this land for Christ Jesus.

I had a new experience of Jesus while at the conference and I wrote the following paragraph to describe what I saw:

> *In a vision I saw the heavens being rolled back and then I went up on to a cloud. I saw the Word go forth and as it did, it changed the cloud as if the sound waves had moved it. Then the cloud turned to gold and the air was like gold. I breathed it in and I breathed it out. Then, I was praying and I was asking God to change me again, to break me, mould me and bend me. Then I saw a second vision where Jesus came and sat on the chair in front of me. He then reached out and put His hand on my forehead, covering my eyes while saying, "See". He repeated the word over and over, "See, See, See".*

When I think about it now, I realise that, technically speaking, my eyes were covered by His hand. The only thing that I could see was Him. Perhaps, the next journey for us and for Ireland will be to get a new vision of God, a new vision of His heart. May it be done in Jesus Name!

Chapter Eighteen
From Curses to Blessing

Nendrum, County Down
Reagh Island, County Down
Greyabbey, County Down

The following testimony was given to us by good friends of ours. They had a wonderful experience while following God's leading and, after I heard their testimony, I felt that it was directly linked to the journey that Edith and I had been on. I say this because, for the past few months, God has been speaking to us in detail about Ireland and curses that have come upon us as listed in the second-half of Deuteronomy 28. I believe that these curses are the punishment for nations which refuse to obey God's will. Amazingly, the journey that my friends were taken on had to do with the first half of that very same chapter, which is about the blessings for a nation if the act in obedience to God. So, I asked them if we could insert their testimony here and they graciously accepted.

March 18th 2015

Following a dream on the 17th March, Saint Patrick's Day, the following came about.

This dream was of the land calling me to come to three locations: Nendrum, Reagh Island viewing point and Greyabbey ruins.

1. Nendrum

> In the dream I was asked to come and listen and that's what we did. The dream said for us to come and listen to the land and drink from its wells. After the dream I could still hear the words echo through the day.
>
> My wife and I set out from Bangor to Nendrum Monastery in Comber, County Down. I have been here before on many occasions but this time there was more to learn and see. It was as if the land was speaking to us. We sang over the place and prayed and then remained in silence to listen. First God showed me the homes and wealthy estates and God told me that they had no right to the land and that this land is His to give. I could hear the crackling of firewood burning nearby. As I turned I was drawn to an area on the outside of the ruins where I found a well. I had been here so many times and I never knew it had a well. This was something that the dream had pointed out, that there was a well. I prayed there and as I prayed I saw it fill up with water to the point you could draw a cup of water from it. I called my wife over to the well and she said that it would fill up and overflow. She said this without knowing my previous thought of the well filling up.
>
> As I prayed over the area I felt a radiating love as if there had been love present in this place before, a community in Christ. People must have praised and worshipped God here before in a true manner.
>
> When we went to leave we felt God telling us to walk through the doorway of the ruins. As we walked through we could feel

the Holy Spirit moving and we experienced the feeling of passing from old to new like leaving the old behind and stepping into a new world leaving the old world behind.

We departed from that place.

2. Reagh Island viewing point

This is a spectacular and scenic place. The presence of the Holy Spirit became tangible and I had a vision of Saint Patrick baptising in the waters right where we were standing. We came across a bridge and then saw what looked like a throne under a big tree. We felt an increase of God's presence at the bridge and again at the throne. Again we prayed and listened.

To recap, first we saw an overflowing well, then a bridge, then a door leading from old to new and now a throne with a great tree above it.

As we were leaving, we looked into the field on the other side away from the water. The trees there were in the shape of the word "Hell". We both saw it and were amazed. I had a feeling that the third place could be even more interesting.

3. Greyabbey ruins, Greyabbey

We travelled to the other side of Strangford Lough to the ruins that I saw in my dream.

As soon as we got out of the car we felt fear in the atmosphere as we overlooked the ruins. The site was locked up. There was a horrible, stressful noise of crows in the air and around the trees and ruins. I took a video of the birds and the noise and was shocked when I looked back over it as the tree in the video resembled a beast with its mouth open ready to bite and the church lay within its reach of biting. When we went near the ruined church, God showed us that that church had been built on pride and was more of a monument to men than an altar to God and its ruin was due to pride. We rebuked the place and *left.*

Here is a list of what we read and saw:

1. *Deuteronomy 28.*

2. *An overflowing well.*

3. *A doorway from old to new.*

4. *A bridge (we really felt the power of God here. It was like a place of union as in marriage).*

5. *A throne under a tree. The tree was ready to bloom. It was a tree ready to burst into life. The throne would be plentiful, one that would be shaded by the trees. Shadow: 'Rest in the shadow of the Lord Almighty'.*

6. *Vision of St Patrick baptising (this was an awesome picture).*

7. *Trees in the shape of the word 'Hell'.*

8. *A beast, full of pride devouring the church and causing fear.*

9. *Deuteronomy 28:1-14 NIV (see below)*

"If you fully obey the Lord your God and carefully follow all his commands I give you today, the Lord your God will set you high above all the nations on earth. All these blessings will come on you and accompany you if you obey the Lord your God: You will be blessed in the city and blessed in the country. The fruit of your womb will be blessed, and the crops of your land and the young of your livestock—the calves of your herds and the lambs of your flocks. Your basket and your kneading trough will be blessed. You will be blessed when you come in and blessed when you go out. The Lord will grant that the enemies who rise up against you will be defeated before you. They will come at you from one direction but flee from you in seven. The Lord will send a blessing on your barns and on everything you put your hand to. The Lord your God will bless you in the land he is giving you.

The Lord will establish you as his holy people, as he promised you on oath, if you keep the commands of the Lord your God and walk in obedience to him. Then all the peoples on earth will see that you are called by the name of the Lord, and they will fear you. The Lord will grant you abundant prosperity—in the fruit of your womb, the young of your livestock and the crops of your ground—in the land he swore to your ancestors to give you. The Lord will open the heavens, the storehouse of his bounty, to send rain on your land in season and to bless all the work of your hands. You will lend to many nations but will borrow from none. The Lord will make you the head, not the tail. If you pay attention to the commands of the Lord your God that I give you this day and carefully follow them, you will always be at the top, never at the bottom. Do not turn aside from any of the commands I give you today, to the right or to the left, following other gods and serving them." [Deuteronomy 28:1-14 NIV]

Rodney & Rosa Burton

I think that Rodney and Rosa's experience is very important. History records that Nendrum was founded by a disciple of St Patrick; it therefore dates back to the start of God's move in Ireland. Nendrum was most likely destroyed when the Anglo-Normans came to Ireland in the 12th century and it was they who established the church at Greyabbey. What I believe God was saying is that, in the beginning, there was a huge spiritual well in Ireland that was like fire (Rodney heard a fire that brought him to the well). God is telling us that now is the time to pass beyond everything that has gone before in our history and enter into something new. We must walk through the door of the unknown and never turn back. We must never come back to the religion, the barren place and be subject to the curses. On the other side of that door is a bridge that we must cross. Beyond it we will find Jesus seated on His throne. He sits there waiting for us and, when we reach Him, each one of us will carry such an anointing that we will have a ministry with more impact than Patrick's because we will be following Jesus alone. Our lives will reveal Jesus, the One who leads us. It is as if He were a rider and we his horse and we moved together in unison. Under His tree, we find shade from the pride that had eaten up the former church. We will not follow the path of religiousness any more because that road leads to hell and our Irish history is a testimony to that fact!

This has been a truly wonderful story, the story of a land and a people deeply loved by God who, unfortunately, turned away from Him but are now returning to Him. As we finish this part of a much greater story, the words of this verse remain as our prayer for Ireland:

> "Satisfy us in the morning with your unfailing love, that we may sing for joy and be glad all our days. Make us glad for as many days as you have afflicted us, for as many years as we have seen trouble. May your deeds be shown to your servants, your splendour to their children. May the favour of the Lord our God rest on us; establish the work of our hands for us— yes, establish the work of our hands." [Psalm 90:14-17 NIV]

Chapter Nineteen
Identifying religious spirits

What we have seen throughout this book is how the devil has used man-made religion to cause havoc in our lives and in our country. I remember years ago how I sought God for the spiritual gift of discernment which is something that all of us should pray and ask God for as it helps us not to be deceived. I'll give you an example of how it helped us. About a year ago, Edith and I went to visit some friends of hers who now attended a different church. They invited us to come along and so we went. However, as soon as we were inside the building, both of us felt that something was not right. Everything felt weird, from the literature to the background music. When the service started, things got even worse and they did things that shocked me. Yet, the whole event remained almost believable because of their active testimonies. There were things that happened during that meeting that helped us discern that something was wrong. For example, instead of having wine and bread for communion, they just had water. They also talked about holding another meeting where they would have milk and honey while simultaneously bringing things from their homes to leave at the altar. That meeting was going to be held the following Friday, Friday the 13th.

I have to say that, because of how we felt, we didn't take part in anything that they did. We didn't sing or pray with them and we didn't take anything that they offered us. Eventually I prayed and said, "Lord, reveal to me what is going on here". I immediately saw, in a vision, three eyes and they were on three walls. I did not understand this at the time but we still decided to leave. Even leaving was a strange process where people had to get permission to leave. We walked out, praying and rebuking the spirits that were operating in the place. Later on, I did an internet search for a three-eyed god and what I found astounded me. The three-eyed god was a demon which killed its own. Therefore, if a person had a spirit of oppression on them, this three-eyed god would kill it in order to gain that person's allegiance and following. This immediately explained the 'testimonies' that we had heard at the church as they seemed to have been very convincing accounts of people being set free. I looked deeper into what this religion did. In a list of ceremonies honouring the three-eyed god was a special ceremony that was always held on the 13th of the month, where people would bring offerings from their homes to leave at the altar and then drink milk and honey! I was amazed. Then I was thankful to God for giving me discernment but I was also sorrowful because I knew that people had become trapped in this demonic religion which claimed to proclaim Jesus and Christianity. I don't know which Jesus they were talking about. It certainly wasn't my Jesus!

I will say that, while discernment may not be given to everyone, it can be very helpful in specific situations. I think that religious spirits who operate through the minds of religious people can prove to be very difficult to identify. How do we know if a religious spirit is involved? Perhaps we are dealing with a person who is very religious and traditional in their thinking. Perhaps, this has happened because of how they were brought up or for some other unknown reasons. Discernment involves the application of a certain amount of wisdom and caution. For instance, God might reveal a spirit to you that is actively working in a church but not want you do anything about it straightaway. This certainly happened to me on at least one occasion. Later on, I was brought back to the information I had received to pray about the matter at the right time, as the Holy Spirit led me. Discernment in the hands of someone who does not use wisdom and caution can lead to disaster. It could even tear a church asunder. Wisdom is required and not our wisdom but God's. I would certainly not wish for anyone to take any of the information in this section of the book and use it in an unwise way or use it without applying God's love.

What we have learned in this journey is that religious spirits in Ireland have been very active. While you could meet a man who is seventy years old and set in his ways but does not try to apply his rigid religion to others, you need to realise, that is simply not how religious spirits work. Religious spirits take the man-made ideas we already have and use them to infect others. This is the 'yeast of the Pharisees' that Jesus talked about. It is an active agent that infiltrates those who come into contact with it. The truth is, all of us have already come into contact with it and have already been contaminated with the 'yeast of the Pharisees'. In each of us, it exists in varying amounts. Some of us who have recognised its presence have already begun to process of casting it out of our hearts. I don't believe that this is a process that can be completed overnight because many of us have been in contact with man-made religion ever since we were children. We need to try our best to cast it away, but more importantly, we must ensure that no part of that 'yeast of the Pharisees' touches the next generation. We want to prevent them from being laden down with such a thing. That, brothers and sisters is our goal. It is for us to seek God for freedom from man-made religion and to actively protect the next generation from it.

With any disease, doctors tell us that prevention is better than the cure. If we avoid smoking then the chance of developing lung cancer is less. If we get the flu vaccination then we will be less likely to get the flu. We have seen on this journey how man-made religion is a kind of sickness that infiltrates the hearts and minds all of us. So therefore, if we can prevent that happening in our children, what a wonderful achievement that would be! Think about the changes that take place from generation to generation. For example, my parent's generation were never given the measles vaccination and therefore suffered with the disease, whereas in my generation, we got the vaccination and most of us were saved from having to endure it. One generation needs to stand and proclaim, "My son or my daughter, will not be infected with that disease". That generation will of course be heavily dependent on doctors and pharmaceutical companies for the medical knowledge needed for the creation and presentation of the vaccines. Similarly, spiritually speaking, what we need is knowledge but we are totally dependent on God for it. It is only Jesus who can truly set us free.

Here are questions to ask which will help identify if religious spirits are at work:

1. Is it a place where claims of grandeur / gifting / miracles /events / music occur? [Then 'yeast of Pharisees' is at work]
2. Is it a place where there are rules that restrict the moving of God's Spirit? [Then 'yeast of Pharisees' is at work]
3. Is it place where disputes are handled without love? [Then division is occurring]
4. Is it place where believers do not mature? [Then there is a loss of inheritance occurring]
5. Is it a place where dependence is not on God, and there are signs of it from the leadership right through to the congregation? [Then rebellion against God is occurring]
6. Is it a place where the children and/or the women are expected to keep quiet? [Then spiritual slavery is occurring]
7. Is it a place where leaders are put 'on a pedestal' and the congregation cannot challenge them? [Then pride is at work]
8. Is it a place where 'church' is performed but there is a lack of spiritual fruit and a lack of sustenance? [Then spiritual famine is occurring]
9. Is it a place where there is a hardness of heart, where no tears are shed, where emotions are restrained and real love is not shared? [Then people have a heart of stone]

I want to make it clear that this is in no way meant to judge any person or church. The simple truth is that that there might be no church that is free of all of these things. One church may struggle with pride, while another may struggle with bringing people to maturity. Our hope in God is that right across this land that new ministries and churches will arise, that are set free from the control of man-made religion. For all those which are already established, recognising a problem and then bringing it before God is very different from ignoring it and allowing it to continue. When we read the letters written to the churches in the Book of Revelation, we can see that churches right from the beginning experienced challenges which needed to be overcome. Our task is to find a way forward that will both protect and establish the next generation so that they can accomplish what God has prepared for them. Whether or not you choose to listen and seek God about the answers is your responsibility.

The Promised Land is referred to several times in the Bible. From Deuteronomy we learn that once we have crossed into our promised land, defeated the enemy and settled there, we should remain vigilant and obey everything God tells us. Most of the time, we get this mixed up. We hear the call of God, perhaps the call to become a worship leader but then we add in our own ideas such as recording music or having a Youtube channel. Was it right for us to add on our own things to our original calling? We need to bring everything to God for His approval. Why? Because He tell us to do so! When God speaks, our responsibility is to hear Him and obey. Nothing else! I'll leave you with this one last verse and I hope and pray that you will realise how important it is to fully obey God's commands:

> "See that you do all I command you; do not add to it or take away from it." [Deuteronomy 12:22 NIV]

MIKE HARPER

Research sources

[1] *The Story of Ireland*, TV documentary for BBC and RTE, 2011

[2] *The World of Saint Patrick* by Philip Freeman, Oxford University Press, 2014 [ISBN-13: 978-0199372584]

[3] *A History of the Irish Church* by John R Walsh & Thomas Bradley [ISBN-13: 978-1856074025]

[4] The Columba Press, 1991 *Labor Gabala Erenn: The Book of the Taking of Ireland* by Robert Alexander & Stewart Macalister, Dublin University Press, 1939

[5] [Confederate oath of association] MS 812, fols 243r-243v held at Trinity College Dublin

[6] *God has a Wonderful Plan for Your Life: The Myth of the Modern Message* by Ray Comfort, Living Waters Publications, 2010.

[7] Certain acts and declarations made by the ecclesiastical Congregation of the Archbishops, Bishops, and other Prelates met at Clonmacnoise, the 4th day of December 1649, together with a declaration of the Lord Lieutenant of Ireland, Cork, 1649.

[8] *The Muster Roll of the County of Donnagall,* as printed in the Donegal Annual, A.D. 1630.

[9] *An historical account of the plantation in Ulster: 1608-1620* by Rev. George Hill, 1877.

[10] *The Magdalene Sisters*, a 2002 film by Peter Mullan.

[11] *A Chronological Listing of Early Weather Events* by James A. Marusek https://wattsupwiththat.files.wordpress.com/2011/09/weather1.pdf

[12] *Be Revived: Prophecies & Revelations*, by CESAR [ISBN-13: 978-1481863070]

[13] 'The Healing Power of Afflictions' sermon by David Wilkerson http://youtu.be/pp0n5RjBHKw

[14] *In Spirit and Truth*, by CESAR [ISBN-13: 978-1497308053]

15 *Be Revived: Open the Box*, by CESAR [ISBN-13: 1484065484]

16 *The Harvest is Here*, by CESAR [ISBN-13: 978-1503141131]

17 *'The Cost of a Fresh Anointing'* sermon by David Wilkerson http://youtu.be/0vmE2nbVctE

18 *'A Call to Anguish'* sermon by David Wilkerson http://youtu.be/q-CFMN3wDPo

19 *'Seeds for the Journey'* [ISBN-13: 978-1503321618]

OTHER BOOKS BY THE AUTHOR

Prayers, Poems Songs

Book of Prophecies

Be Revived *Prophecies & Revelations*

Be Revived *Open the Box*

Revival Prayers

Edify *Dreams Prophecies & Visions*

Faith Beyond Miracles

Calling the Bride Calling the Church

In Spirit and Truth

Prayers Prophecies Dreams

The Harvest is Here

A Letter to the End Times Church

A Remnant Hope

Made in the USA
Charleston, SC
02 December 2015